bardo times

BEAUTIFUL TRAITOR BOOKS

bardo times

hyperreality

high-velocity

simulation

automation

mutation

a hoax?

Kingsley L. Dennis

Published by Beautiful Traitor Books – http://www.beautifultraitorbooks.com/

ISBN-13: 978-1-9999053-5-4 (paperback)

First published: 2018

Front Cover & Book Design – Ibolya Kapta

info@beautifultraitorbooks.com

Acknowledgements: Thanks to John Tintera for all our bardo chats over the recent years. Humour is a good antidote for the human spirit.

DEDICATION

For everyone who wishes to see beyond

CONTENTS

introduction

There's something going on, but you don't know what it is –

do you, Mr Jones?

Bob Dylan

Now for something different.

Previously I have written about the disenchantment of the world, and of our dis-coupling from a dynamic, creative cosmos, and how this disenchantment is on course to be overturned by an emerging revival of the sacred.[1] I have written about the rise of participatory consciousness, feminine energy and soul, and a new kind of 'magic communion' creeping through our technologies. In other words, my previous work examined the positive road toward which we could be heading if the ensuing years turn out to our benefit. But of course...what if?

[1] *The Sacred Revival: Magic, Mind & Meaning in a Technological Age* (SelectBooks, 2017)

There are also other roads, potentialities, and possibilities. And getting a foot on the right road ahead means taking the right first steps. Those early steps may keep us in a not-too-pleasant state for a number of years. And so I felt compelled to examine the current and likely ongoing sense of malaise, eerie disquiet, and the alienated soul at work in today's hype and hyperreality. There is a battle for our attention going on; a seemingly deliberate attempt to distract us from ourselves and from our awareness of the real goings-on in the world around us.

Our cultures reflect our shared reality, and what we take to be our 'reality' is the indefinable field that marks our boundaries. It is these boundaries and these shared beliefs that we use to keep us sane. It is not so important what people know or think – or believe they know – so much as what people feel deep within them. What matters is how we feel and sense the world around us, and how we use this to distinguish between what is the 'real' and what is fantasy. Once this demarcation begins to break down, then we start to lose our moorings. We are set adrift, and in this drifting space we accept, or rather allow, things to happen that we would not normally. This is the uncertainty period, and these times can lend themselves to a lot of wild speculations as well as a mix of the spectacular with the fear-mongering. It is my sense that we are passing through one of these rifts right in this moment. That is why I felt compelled in this book to examine at the ever-present now.

We are at the end of something, and endings naturally bring with them their illusions, as well as their delusions. We are being thrust into a new era that is quite literally beyond both the modern and the postmodern. As such, we are also being thrust into a space that has not yet formed. It is in this space in which we now find ourselves. It is a space where, as if in seeming contradiction, we encounter the space-less. And it is a time where we encounter the time-less. Simultaneously, the context of our reality around us appears to be both speeding up and speeding away. The result is a sense of the hyperreal; of the 'once real' now becoming a simulation.

The notions of hyperreality and simulation/ simulacra were both concepts explored within postmodern theory. It was considered that our perceptions were unable to distinguish reality from a simulation of reality, especially in technologically advanced societies. And this is more or less where we still are, only deeper within the transition between significant social eras. Or to use a Buddhist term, we are in what is referred to in the Tibetan language as bardo. That is, we are in an 'in-between' or 'liminal state' which is said to exist between lives. In the context in which I use it here, it refers to the state between epochs; hence, a transitional state as we leave behind one social era and push through into the new.

In this transitional phase, events follow a non-linear path in that they can follow a curve, be bendy, complex, fractals, and a whole kaleidoscope of mixtures. And this non-linearity is what is blurring many of the bounds, binds, and binaries that form our picture of reality. That's why it may seem for many of us that we, or our societies, are in freefall. This is the illusion, and yet it is also terrifyingly real. On the one hand it is a simulation, and on the other it is a substitute reality that we have to contend with until an updated one is formed. We are experiencing the liquid, fluid stages between all the jumbled moments. This liquidity announces a transformation in our perceptions of reality and new modalities of thought. This is not 'modernity' - this is something entirely else. We are going beyond history and into a future of unprecedented change and flux. And in such fluid space no true linearity exists.

Reality – whatever that may be - is something that exists and yet in which we do not believe.

As a writer I am a work of fiction. I'm not real in the sense of a thing of flesh and blood. I am a regurgitator of ideas that are already floating out there. As a writer I am not the me who eats his breakfast, scratches his behind, and blows his nose. Likewise, this book doesn't deal with the you in your everyday situations. I don't know what personal issues any of you, the readers, have; nor of your very real physical lives. Yet this book is about the seas in which we all swim in. Not all waters are alike, however; some are muddier than others. But there is something creeping through all the seas. In some way or another, we can each be affected by what is going on through these waters of reality that surround us on all sides. It may be subtle; just something that splashes in, or it may be more brutal as it washes over us. Yet at the very least we need to be aware of these possibilities, potentials, and presences.

I don't defend. I observe and describe.

We are in the throes of moving from one era to another. Some commentators say that we are shifting from the postmodern into something else – that is, we are pre-something. Perhaps we are lingering as lost souls from the post to the pre, which is between lives and this is exactly where the bardo realm lies – after one life and before the next to come. And it is a realm we are always faced with crossing, whether by soul or by the social.

In those times that mark the transition of our eras the power of myth and stories are prevalent. We are the stories we choose to live within. And those stories that we choose to tell ourselves become the reality myth that guides us. This book is about how those stories and myths are not only affecting our sense of reality but also how they are being directly utilized to further blur the distinction between reality and fiction. There is so much deliberate play now going on with the 'senses of reality.'

Those things that have guided us for so long as stable bodies are now being cut-up and pasted and re-presented to us in a manner that confuses. At the same time, we are also jumping into the foray by buying into this play and amplifying it. We are the players upon the stage, strutting our stuff and ad-libbing our lines. Modern life appears as a contradiction – it is both in our faces as well as eerily distant from us.

This book dissects modern life because such life deserves it – modern life is itself fragmented, fractalized, and begging for observers to observe it to bring it into being. Or, in the words of quantum physics, we act to collapse the wave form to bring some semblance of reality into being. And that more or less sums it up – we seem to be living within vast waves that wash over us and through us and which, for many of us, are invisible. They collapse into being around us through our perceptions, our recognition and, most dangerously of all, through our acceptance and acquiescence.

There are certain positions and observations I have made yet maybe not everything I say in this book is absolutely true. That is because nothing can be really that true when discussing modern life. Some things I may have emphasized in order to make a point rather than attempting to claim its veracity. And that's the nature of this book; it was penned to make both the potential reader and myself to think. Things may not be all that bad, but in the short term we really do need to get a good grip on some issues and to scrutinize them from various positions. That's why I've taken this road trip through some of our modern cultures, memes, issues, and twisted quirks and irks. We really should be on the lookout. The layers of delusion are getting deeper as they are growing subtler – the illusion of the rabbit hole is an impressive one. And then there's the other part of it – namely us. Are we not collectively playing the part of the somnambulists, the sleepwalkers? But not to worry - we have the mutant super-heroes and the bubble-gum-flavored pop.

At the end of each chapter I have also indulged in a divine chat. That is, I have called upon one of the gods to enter into a short dialogue with me – what I refer to as a Bardo Chat – in order to help elucidate some points. These gods are clever folks, and they always leave me with something to ponder. They were kind enough to pander to my call at each chapter end, for which I am grateful. There, I have admitted it – this book was not a singular affair. I had a little help from my friends.

Finally, I wish to say that each chapter of this book could have been a whole book in itself. That is, each chapter subject has enough potential to stretch it out into an extended investigation. Yet I have chosen to make a whirlwind trip through each of these themes as self-contained chapters that are explorative yet brief. If you, the reader, require more food for your mind, then the rest of the homework is in your hands. I wanted to touch upon each chapter subject just enough to make some salient points and to steer the spotlight into some cultural corners. I never expected to make this journey a complete one, for it is only an adventurous beginning into a modern jungle of jugglers, gigglers, and Gnostic wranglers. And everything starts with a beginning, just like this...

Kingsley L. Dennis
Casa Roja, Al-Andalus
April 2018

1.
haunted lives
our incomparable sense of loss

1. haunted lives – our incomparable sense of loss

ˈhɔːntɪd/

adjective

(of a place) frequented by a ghost.

showing signs of mental anguish or torment.

'We can now recognize that the fate of the soul is the fate of the social order; that if the spirit within us withers, so too will all the world we build about us.'

Theodore Roszak, *Where the Wasteland Ends*

Queen Victoria,
The Twentieth Century belongs to you and me.
Let us be two severe giants not less lonely for our partnership,
Who discolor test tubes in the halls of Science,
Who turn up unwelcome at every World's Fair,
Heavy with proverbs and corrections,
Confusing the star-dazed tourists
With our incomparable sense of loss.

Leonard Cohen, *Queen Victoria*

The incomparable sense of loss that Cohen's lonely protagonists feel seems to mirror our own current twenty-first century predicament. The difference is that the loss is not only lingering within us but also without in our external lives. It lingers around us like a haunting, an indistinguishable dream. The modern age with its technological achievements were intended to bring about an age of discovery, in the spirit and hope of sharing our new golden dream. The physical world was being brought closer together into a common fate that heralded a fellowship of humanity. We were discovering new tools to redraw the portrait of the collective human face. And all this has had a profound effect upon the human psyche. The ability to share an experience globally amongst our brethren brought about such power that has released psychic forces within us. And yet many of us can see and witness disturbances and distress in our societies that do not have shared interests at heart. We notice this conflict, and react to it, both on a conscious as well as unconscious level. And this great contradiction weighs upon us and affects us in ways not fully known. In our great need to have an authentic experience of the world we find ourselves in contention with other forces. And for the greater part these forces impede upon us externally from our societies and cultures. Rather than aiding and nurturing we find many social obstacles in our way. On the other side, if we choose not to challenge or question our situation then we are provided with an endless range of high-gloss entertainment to satiate us. The world we inhabit exists for many of us like a theatrical puppet play.

Over the course of history we have attempted to map the world, to frame and understand it, as it shifts from one hypothesis or grand narrative and into another. The world as we know it has gone from being flat to round; from being the center of the universe to the center of the solar system; from being animistic and supernatural to raw in tooth and claw; from being particle-atomic to wavy-quantum. And now we are disappearing into the digital domains of virtual-augmented spaces and false information, bombarded with the spectacle and the image. And somewhere in the midst of all this is the human condition, the elephant that sits in the corner of the room. If there's a crime here, then it is that we've allowed ourselves to become haunted – to live haunted lives that lack significance and meaning. The 'objects' or values that we have attempted to live by, or that we pursue - such as power, truth, understanding, dreams, work, love, and the rest - have all seemingly vanished into some warped, elusive reality where the presence of these things no longer tangibly exist. However, the doubt, uncertainty, and pain of their absence – or 'fake presence' – are indeed real enough to affect us deeply. We seek the substitutes for what has already disappeared.

We are now close to where we are acting out our fantasies upon the phantasmal theatre of our lives and thinking it is reality. This theatre, or screen, of fantasies and the fantastical is like the cave wall in Plato's allegory where the flickering shadows that move across are taken to be the real. In an updating of Plato's famous allegory, we no longer have shadows projected upon the cave wall; they are now projected upon the green screens that form the back-drop for computer-generated imagery (CGI) that adorn our movies, television programs, and video games. Within this encroaching visual world, full of misinformation that influences our worldview, we are made to believe in a different kind of reality. It is a reality that is uncertain and insecure, and that requires for us to hold deep obedience to our state institutions to protect us. And within this projection of reality, meanings are provided for us as ready-made meals. In other words, full of too much salt, saturated fats, and laziness.

These socially manufactured meanings are provided as a substitute for the genuine lack. Of these choices offered we often take our pick, as consumers in a marketplace. It may be career, wealth, fame, achievement, or a combination of these and more. Yet the manufactured consent in our sense of meaning, no matter how thoroughly pursued, is still not genuine. And like the ready-made meal, it soon leaves us with a continued hunger. We can say that the world we have come to know is a great spectacle of illusion and play; of movement, distraction, simulation, and excess. Yet rather than critically confronting the illusions and distractions we are cleverly persuaded to indulge in them. The world has become a lot more complex as it has moved toward greater connectivity. The world we share now is also shared with our collective doubts, fears, anger, and frustrations. And these new emotions upon the global stage are blurring our picture of the world and its future. Whilst we may be excited and genuinely inspired by this increased complexity and diversity there has also been a cultural backlash, in the western nations especially. That is, we have witnessed a false simplicity through generic news, bland reporting, and excruciatingly trivial entertainment. This clash of the complex with the simple is creating an odd reality where things just don't feel right anymore.

The result is that our sense of collective reality is going through a quantum 'collapse mode' into an altogether stranger reality. And this is what I refer to as the bardo times - a surreal liminal state between different social eras. And the consequence of this fluidity and uncertainty is a hauntingness. It is, as the original definition says, a mental and emotional anguish. It is also combined with a sense of our unsure futures, making for an odd mix of nostalgic anguish with future uncertainty. We have met with our own realm of the haunted.

It is similar to the figure of a ghost; a specter that is neither present, nor absent, neither dead nor alive. For us, in the here and now, our haunted state is where there is a longing, mixed with nostalgia, for a sense of our unknown, ephemeral futures. It calls out for those futures that we once thought were right there, almost touching our fingertips; but they fell away from our grasp. Where did they go? How did we lose them? The futures promised to us have seeped into a bardo realm where hyperreality, high-velocity, and simulation are making a new and unpredictable mix. It is a realm where talks of the technological singularity mesh with artificial intelligence, augmented reality, nanotech, nano-biology, and mind-numbing entertainment.[1] This is the waking bardo that we have to cross in order to reach the other side. It will be a ride through the flippant and the flimsy, the significant and the necessary, as we are expected to find our foothold – our very human soul – in a world seemingly on the verge of insanity. In such a world, Disneyland may seem to some as the greatest of sanctuaries; whilst to the rest of us it stands as a superficial sign of our times. But for how much longer?

The hauntingness that surrounds us today is breaking up our known and mapped mindscapes, imaginary lands, visual cartographies, and future visions. It is taking apart almost all of what we took to be our territories and is re-arranging them. The sacred totems that signified our social realities for so long are on the move. Everything is on the move. It is an almost impossible task to map these mutations.

---

[1] For technological singularity, see - https://en.wikipedia.org/wiki/Technological_singularity

The current state of our lives is such that we are now faced with a pace of change so fast that events behind us very quickly seem so far away. Can many of us today imagine a life when we didn't have our mobile phones or the internet? We have only had the internet as a public domain for a little over two decades, and yet pre-internet life is almost impossible to remember. Our environments of social interaction, our mediums of communication and ways of expression, and the very way of doing things have shifted at an incredible pace. And this pace of change shows no signs of slowing down. Every time we make a move forward we appear to erase a part of our past. Yet there are perhaps some aspects of our past, of our historical path, that we are meant to lose and to let go of. And some of these aspects concern our perspectives and ways of thinking; our models of reality – of life, the universe, and everything, as they say – and those older paradigms that govern our social and cultural institutions. Going forward is always about leaving certain things behind, which inevitably causes its own confusion.

History has a habit of trying to retain what it believes to be authentic. It tells us that events occurred that were 'actual authentic events' and these were then recorded – or frozen – for posterity. We grow up among our specific cultural stories and narratives of history, believing that everything happened exactly as recorded. And we also grow up believing that each event starts out as authentic. In literary theory the act of believing the authenticity of a story, even if within us we know it could not have happened the way it is told, is referred to as the willing suspension of disbelief. We drop our disbelief in order to allow ourselves to accept the story. Oddly enough, most of us have been doing this for so long that we are accustomed to not questioning our disbelief anymore – rather, we accept everything. The absence of critical disbelief not only feels normal it actually feels 'so right.' Yet any reasonable observer has to admit that history is a biased story. It often chooses to tell a certain perspective, depending on where, and by whom, the history is being written. A simplistic example is that an historical account of a war will be seen, and interpreted differently, according to each side. Official accounts, especially those given approval by the ruling authority/ government/state, will become the 'accepted truth' whether it happened like that or not. Let's face it, history is an unreliable narrator. And just like the unreliable narrator in Ken Kesey's classic book One Flew Over the Cuckoo's Nest (1962), Chief Bromden tells us that, 'it's the truth, even if it never happened.' More recently, this position of historical authenticity was questioned by the French philosopher Jean Baudrillard who wrote The Gulf War Did Not Take Place (1991). We have entered a period where events are presented to us, mostly through image and media re-telling and representations, as the 'official reality.' And this offers up so many questions to us, as I explore further in this book.

As I write this first draft (April 2017) there is a media war raging over the alleged use of chemical weapons – sarin nerve gas – by the Syrian government upon its own citizens. I say 'alleged' because nobody knows the real facts.[2] In England the BBC refer to it as the 'suspected chemical attack' whilst some news agencies in the US refer to it either as 'alleged' or outright Syrian chemical attack. And whilst President Trump is talking about all those 'beautiful babies' in Syria as suffering from chemical attack, where is the evidence for their side of the 'story'? Is this any different from the mainstream news story in 1990 that told of how during Iraq's invasion of

2 As I came to make a final revision, the same strategy of using an 'alleged' chemical attack by the Syrian regime again is being pushed by the western powers. This is exactly one year later, April 2018.

Kuwait, Iraqi soldiers had entered a Kuwaiti hospital and taken babies out of their incubators, stolen the incubators, and left hundreds of babies to die. This testimony was given before the Congressional Human Rights Caucus on October 10, 1990 by a 15-year-old girl who provided only her first name, Nayirah (hence known as the Nayirah Testimony).[3] This testimony was highly publicized across all mainstream news channels and President George H.W. Bush used this rationale at the time to back Kuwait in the ensuing Gulf War. Two years later, in 1992, it was revealed that the 15-year-old Nayirah was in fact the daughter of Saud Al-Sabah, the Kuwaiti ambassador to the United States. Further, it was revealed that her testimony was not only false but was organized as part of the Citizens for a Free Kuwait public relations campaign which was run by an American public relations company (Hill & Knowlton) on behalf of the Kuwaiti government. The Nayirah Testimony has since come to be regarded as a classic example of 'modern atrocity propaganda,' which constitutes psychological warfare. Are we seeing a reoccurring pattern here? Everything seems to make a little less nonsense when we come to

---

[3] See https://en.wikipedia.org/wiki/Nayirah_(testimony)

realize that the vast majority of our mainstream media views form part of a society's 'unreliable narrator.' Yet again, the majority of mainstream viewers have been seduced into the 'willing suspension of disbelief' mode.

Whilst many of us do not have the capacity to verify the truth claims of the mainstream media we are yet more than willing to accept the veracity of their claims. We suspend our own disbelief by trusting in others, especially when it comes to authority and experts. We have been conditioned to respect the positions of authority and 'the expert,' often without critical thought. Documentary film-maker Adam Curtis discusses this phenomenon of how the mainstream media projects a simplified, fake reality in his film HyperNormalization (2016). [4] The term hypernormaliztion was taken from an account of life in the Soviet Union during the twenty years before it collapsed. In this account everyone knew the system was failing but they couldn't envision any alternative and so everyone was resigned to maintaining the pretence of a functioning society. Over time this delusion became accepted as real; an effect termed as hypernormalization. That is, when the fake is finally accepted as the real then we are living in a

---

[4] http://www.imdb.com/title/tt6156350/. The documentary is also available for free download on various internet sites.

hypernormalized state. Does this sound familiar?

The question is – does Reality ever take place?

Our bodies of authority, our mainstream media channels and our centres of learning – that is, a majority of our significant institutions – have turned, or are in the process of turning, into advertising gimmicks. They peddle publicity and propaganda as endless programs stuck on a loop. They serve to produce the appearance of reality; yet they fail to represent a sense of reality. And this fundamental difference has produced a feeling of living haunted lives. We wander as ghosts in liminal zones, in wastelands as gaunt figures hungry for meaning.[5]

In this sense of loss, we no longer seem to know, or distinguish, between oppositions. Almost all our value systems are based on relative terms – good, bad, my history, your history, etc. Often, the values we take to be 'our values' were inculcated in us depending upon which culture we happened to be born into. It is true there are some values more universally shared – such as thou shalt not kill – but the majority of them are culturally relative.

[5] Liminal state is the English translation of Bardo in Tibetan Buddhism.

Take for instance, sex before marriage – good or bad? Same-sex partnerships? Freedom of religious speech? Eating pork? Eating rats? Democrats or Republicans? Labour or Conservative? Which is good, and which is bad? In the case of political parties, it is neither – they are false oppositions. More than that, they are also distractions. When you're arguing (sorry, debating) over political parties you are not observing the system behind them that created this false lack of choice in the first place. False oppositions plague our haunted hinterland. We don't see this if we are the aimless ghosts, or the walking dead. It's not pleasant – it's eerie. And we are in eerie times.

Modernity in its current form is haunted by a sense of loss; of not knowing where it is heading. There are a great many aspects of our age that are in disruption and dislocation. All forms of stability are in question; old and incumbent patterns and models are in dispute; and too many people are experiencing moods of despair and anguish. It is as if our human civilization has come loose from its moorings and is now adrift upon the waters of uncertainty, insignificance, and the loss of meaning. It seems that upon the current path of development our civilization is careering dangerously close to some kind of blind spot where we no longer can tell what is true or false anymore. Truth is replaced by a fake substitute and the false becomes a parody of the truth. And this creates a hyperreality that is also a form of reality crisis (see Chapter Three). There is no real, single tangible form that reality can take, and so it is out-sourced in different forms. One of these forms is the rise of dystopian visions and their movie counterparts; we are in 'catastrophic mode' because all sense of reality is in fractal disarray. And that may be why we are seeing a surge in catastrophe in our popular cultural memes.

The symbols now exploding through our cultural channels no longer hold any essential, core meaning. They represent 'something' whether it is an ideal or idea/ ideology, a notion, a value; yet in themselves they have strayed from their original essence. Many of our cultural symbols are now the shadows of what they once were, and yet we continue to believe that, like the emperor with his new clothes, they remain clothed in significance. And we take them so seriously. In the extreme we are willing to sacrifice ourselves to them or their cause, even unto death. They turn into ineffectual slogans or label stickers, like having 'Make Love Not War – See Driver For Details' stuck on the rear windows of our car. They are the haunted spaces where the mist drifts by. It's like a Zen joke. It's the same as a voice whispering in the darkness saying there is no such thing as a voice whispering in the darkness. They couldn't have written a better riddle if they had tried.

So what went wrong? Where did it all go? What is it, in fact?

A profound sense of unease has crept into many of us, and into our social systems, our cultures, our art, our news, and into the very collective soul of humanity. It is an eeriness; an uncertain disquiet – almost an unsettling foreboding. Something has come loose, and we're not sure what it is. Further still, most of us are fairly certain that those institutions supposedly 'looking after our best interests,' or running the show – whether they be governmental bodies, financial elites, or shadowy organizations and cabals – are not really in control or are sure either. It feels as if something is amiss, and we just can't quite put our finger on it. Welcome to our haunted modernity.

We have for a long time confused ourselves over what constitutes intelligence. Culture has long ingrained in us the notion that power is an expression of intelligence, and that those who wield power must have gotten it through cultivating intelligence. This idea is about as erroneous as the notion that all politicians are good people. These are dysfunctional stereotypes that prey on society and help to build the façade like a gigantic firewall. If an extra-terrestrial race were observing Earth and our diverse societies and cultures, then it would most likely come to the conclusion that stupidity is the foremost attribute of power. It would also probably decide that the human species doesn't know what it wants; doesn't know how to get what it doesn't know it wants; and that political institutions are in position to ensure that people don't have a chance of getting what they don't know they want. Their report may conclude with the words, 'this is why, particularly in chaotic times, citizens will turn in their millions to the person who doesn't ask them to think.'

We are in disarray over almost everything, including climate chaos, stock market panics and economic crashes, offshore tax evasions and leaked documents, political scandals, pandemic threats and contested vaccines, state and terrorist violence, congenital anxiety and existential fear – a whole cauldron of terror, dread, disquiet, nervousness, angst, and collective confusion is bubbling over in many of our societies. We have been infiltrated with a virus and it is infecting not only our bodies but our very minds. The Spanish have a phrase for this state – "de perdidos al río" - and it roughly translates as from lost to the river. That sums it up - we are from lost to the river!

Some have called this reality an illusion ('Maya'), or a delusion (an inversion of the 'Real'). In our current terms we can see it as marketing the banal. One definition of banal is 'so lacking in originality as to be obvious and boring.' And this definition works well for us in that it points to the lack of originality – the copy, the simulation of something genuine. Politics has largely become a grand farce on a world stage; yet unfortunately for the rest of us it has very real consequences which greatly affect our lives. Yet it is played out with cliché characters and often exaggerated social archetypes. Because it is so unreal, so far from reality, it has become an empty form bereft of any genuine goodness or vitality. Thus, it is banal.

We may wonder whether the passion for illusion is greater than our longing for happiness. We are living through a haunting mutation that morphs as it gathers pace. This is the bardo times we are in as we move from one era of civilization to another. It is a stage, and a state, that we should be aware of; and at the same time be wary of becoming too accustomed to.

In such 'haunted lives' we can easily become accustomed to metaphysical anguish as just another everyday pain. It is like a pulled muscle or a sprained ankle; something unpleasant and yet we continue to move around with it. In the end we learn how to project this metaphysical anguish onto other things – we choose intoxicating entertainment, sports, and other cultural pastimes and diversions. There is the danger that we become hypernormalized so that the sense of 'absence of the real' becomes the new reality.

During these bardo times it is essential that we create meaning for ourselves, otherwise the 'distant algorithmic' universe will create for us a deep sense of alienation. In a world of scrambled code and big data, transcendence will seem not within reach or even real. Or, at worse, the very notion of transcendence will seem the delirium of unstable minds. In this instance, transcendence will appear as a form of spiritual autism. And yet the notion of going beyond ourselves, of developing our capacities for higher perception, are the saving grace inherent within our human species. We are incomplete, and this haunts us, and yet it should also give us meaning and a higher aim in life in knowing that there is further to go. We should take comfort in knowing that there are tools within us for creating, shaping, and cultivating these finer faculties. In being haunted we are also being reminded of what is lacking, and this urge should compel us to find a solution within ourselves. We are in fact being 'haunted into remembrance.'

However, for many of us a haunted modernity offers us a conditioned life where there is little or no space for transcendence. There is no other space to move into when life is already haunted and dislocated. In such social and cultural hauntings, there are no navigable locations. We have stepped into an unsouling from the wilderness. Walk on.

A Bardo chat with: Hecate, Greek Goddess of Ghosts

Author (A): Hello Hecate

Hecate (H): Hello there.

A: Thank you for connecting. I would like to begin our talk on the theme of hauntingness. I don't know if that is a real word or not, but these days it seems like these are haunting times we are in.

H: A real word or not, it doesn't matter. I understand your concept. We often sense and feel in concepts, ideas. We don't need the words. Words are ineffective carriers. They are not accurate enough. But words are what you use. So, I need more clarification. What do you mean exactly?

A: Well, as I see it – or perhaps sense it - many people are now feeling somewhat lost. We are in a pace of change so rapid, with distractions, contradictions, misinformation, deliberate false information, and so many things happening around us that it seems reality is losing its focus.

H: Or that people are losing their focus?

A: Exactly. Don't you think so? I mean, this is more your area, where ghosts and phantasms roam the world.

H: Not exactly. The ghosts and phantasms of which you speak are no longer human. The things you mention concerning reality do in fact concern humans. Humans have never, strictly speaking, been my domain. I find them more incomprehensible than ghosts. This is not a bad thing, mind you. Rather, what I am saying is that humans are more complex, unpredictable, and with unknown capacities that they constantly surprise us. What I think is happening right now is that they are in the throes of surprising themselves.

A: What do you mean? Now I have to ask you to clarify!

H: What I mean is that humans are very much at the center of everything they do, and of their world. Things in their world may well be changing, yet it is the humans who decide how this affects them. Humans have more say in their reality than they realize.

A: And isn't this the issue – that they are being misled about their own inherent capacity to act in their world and to create the reality and the future that is best for them?
H: Yes, and this has always been the case. The struggle is not so much with ghosts and hauntings but with their own ignorance. If anything, they are being haunted by their own inability to see. As I said, humans are very much at the center of everything; and it is from this center that they must learn to see clearly.

A: Would you say then that humans are deceiving themselves?

H: Humans have always had a strong inclination for self-deception. This is not always a deliberate act, although it is fascinating to observe from our perspective. This self-deception most often comes from a lack of knowledge; or lack of information about their own state and potential in the world. They are a noble species that step by step, person to person, are moving towards a very different future.

A: And is this a positive, better future?

H: That is indeed the hope.

A: So where do we go from here?

H: We will have to wait and see. Humanity has to make its own choices. And this means it will have to struggle internally - both amongst its own people as well as within each person - to decide how it wishes to act and to move forward.

A: Yet there are also forces acting against humanity, are there not?

H: The forces that concern you and your kind are the ones that exist amongst you. You are your own disease as well as the cure. From what I see, you are struggling with and amongst yourselves. And there are those amongst you who prefer to keep the rest of you in ignorance. Be noble and seek your own truths. The path lies within you, and always has. Don't be distracted by your own ghosts.

A: Are you saying that we have everything we need and that everything is going to work out fine in the end?

H: You are simplifying here and placing into what you call neat categorizations. This is another characteristic of human behavior. Having the tools, you need is not the same as knowing you have them. And knowing you have them is not the same as knowing how to use them. Regarding the future, nothing is fixed. You live more by belief and imagination.

A: Ah yes, thanks. I spoke a little hastily there. Now what do you mean by belief and imagination?

H: Well, nothing in your realms is already as it is. It's difficult to translate this into words. There is being which always is, yet the structures for this - your lives on the planet, your civilization, and your futures - well, these are products of what come from within you. You asked at the beginning about hauntingness as if there was a lack of meaning, or a sense of meaningless. This is a false thing – it simply is not so. Everything is meaning. And so, everything already is meaningful. There is meaning even in false things. Their falsity is itself their meaning. Even when living within ignorance we can take that ignorance as a site for meaning. You must learn to understand things from their fragments. The life you are living, this reality you dwell within, is not perfect by any means. In fact, it is flawed. And yet this imperfection is the realm from where meaning is generated. I would say that your sense of hauntingness is because you have made the visible invisible in your reality. In its place you have made non-important things the visible.

A: Meaning?

H: (laughs) Meaning that the meaning is within you. If there is a lack of meaning in your life it is because you have not brought this meaning forth through yourself.

A: So, it all comes from us?

H: Of course! Where else?

A: Some may say from a Creator God or a similar Divine Source, for example.

H: And what is the Created? If people choose to say that it all comes from a Creator God, then you are this Creation and so this God must work through you. And then we are back to belief and imagination.

A: Ah yes, I had almost forgotten.

H: Forgetting is another major issue of you humans – but let's not get into that here. And why say 'almost forgotten' when you had forgotten? These are all the little deceptions you play with yourselves (laughs). Anyway, I move on. Belief and imagination work in similar ways. You choose an idea or concept and you manifest it. Belief works by being something you want to be true, or to exist; and imagination is something you wish to come true or make happen. They are similar mechanisms and yet they operate in different ways through your mental systems. Belief tends to be used more for blocking than for moving ahead. And imagination tends to be regarded as something not true or not existing even though its purpose is to make something exist. You have confused yourselves with these operations. This is perhaps why you are also confused with meaning. You don't know what gives meaning. You're looking under rocks for the sunlight.

A: Mm, yes. There's a lot to think about there.

H: Don't think on it too much or you'll destroy it! (laughs)

A: You seem to be fairly, well, I don't know exactly how to say it. You're jovial, or joyful for a goddess of ghosts. I expected you'd be more mournful.

H: These are your expectations and have nothing to do with me, thankfully! These are yet again your blocks. You place something in your minds and your group mental sets and then these become like concrete blocks. You walk heavy with such weight in your minds.

A: Yes, I suspect you are right. Thanks for that. And thank you for the chat, Hecate. I've enjoyed it.

H: You're welcome. Goodbye.

2.

unsouling from the wilderness

– becoming quantifiable

2. unsouling from the wilderness – becoming quantifiable

'wɪldənɪs/

noun

an uncultivated, uninhabited, and inhospitable region.
a neglected or abandoned area.
a position of disfavour, especially in a political context.

Crazy Horse dreamed and went into the world where there is nothing but the spirits of all things. That is the real world that is behind this one, and everything we see here is something like a shadow from that one

Black Elk, Black Elk Speaks

Modern man, I dutifully noted, is in search of a soul, and the age is an age of longing.

Theodore Roszak, Where the Wasteland Ends

Perhaps the reason some of us are feeling a sense of loss and longing is that we are, as Black Elk informs us, living in the shadow world. Our reality on this side may only be the fleeting ghosts of a place that is more real somewhere else. On this side we have broken our commitment to the earth and have unsouled ourselves from the wilderness. By the first century CE, the essayist Plutarch was asking, "Why is it that the gods are no longer speaking to us?"

For a long time now, we have been trying to create a new and different image of ourselves. It is an image where modern humanity is placed at the center of its own universe. We learn by observing, probing, experimenting, and finally dissecting and destroying the dynamic world we live within. From this, the modern mind started to develop a new reality for itself.

The collective reality in which we now reside does not take kindly to opposing perspectives. We have inherited an alienated consciousness that views the world as an outside entity - a world of objects that move in mechanical motion. This alienated consciousness has substituted the enchantment and mystery of living within a dynamic and animated world with a dream of the artificial, and ultimately the unreal. The modern landscape is now more scattered with administration than adventure. The central image of our modern age has been that of consumerism: the ability of the average person to buy the material goods they require in order to have a decent standard of living. A standard of living albeit promoted to us through our mainstream media and glamorous propaganda.

Only recently have some of us come to realize that consumerism has now become a contemporary form of crash therapy for unsatisfied people wanting to buy their way into happiness to escape from the very system they are simultaneously supporting. The easy acquisition of things has become more about trying to cover up anxiety as a substitute for contentment. Modern life, especially in the highly-developed West, is now rife with people parading their false selves in place of authenticity.

The modern history of the West has been about the removal of mystery, mind, and magic from the world around us. In the past there were realms of wilderness that existed outside of the social order, and each culture had these 'wild zones' where people danced with the little folk in the woods, undertook initiations in caves, circles, and hard-to-find corners. There were pagan rituals, crazy ecstasies, and unknown zones where primal energies were released. These were the places of wilderness, where dreamtime reigned, and clock-time was banned. And now these wild places are fewer and fewer as a new 'reality order' becomes the manifesto of the day. Now it is many of us who are feeling haunted. We have lost the presence of the 'transcendent' within our modern societies.

We must now recognize that something has happened - a break, a mutation, has occurred that has placed us in an 'intermediate' stage between eras. Modern life is being not so much rewritten as reconfigured. We are seeing odd things occurring in relation to time, speed, and distance. It's as if right now the clock, and our sense of timing, is malfunctioning. This ahistorical period is out of time, until it resets itself. And here, the possibility of transcendence lingers like a phantasma.

We are in a time of carnivalesque distortion where 'fast food' is a parody of our normal food preparation and consumption; mediatized sport is a spectacle of its original form; and the music industry is one huge commercial carnival that mocks genuine creativity.

In the pop music industry, the spectacle, the live show – the 'carnival performance' – is often more important than the actual merit of the song (even when the performer mimes, as they often do). We are in a different world right now – or at least a seemingly different reality.

In this new world of different relations, symbols, and meanings we have become unmoored from our harbors. We are talking about the fractal, the quantum, the molecular, the nano, the bots, artificial intelligence, and the singularity – yet we find we have no soulful connection with any of these terms or their significances. Perhaps we have entered a void-time.

The Sense of the Void

With human life having lost its reference to transcendence and the notion of the sacred, there is the ever-present danger that we may descend to a form of human morality that lacks any real meaning or higher principles. It is not hard to believe that a degree of inertia has crept into our modern societies. The result is that many of us may now be finding ourselves with a hollow space inside. This space becomes the perfect seedbed for the consuming desires, distractions, and attractions of modernity's excesses. Within such an environment we wonder whether we may find ourselves waking up to a world where the dream is still dreaming itself and we can no longer distinguish what is real.

An age of the quantifiable has been ushered in and everyone, and everything, gets given a mark or a measurement. Ever since the industrial age brought in the points system – the marking scores - into mass education we've been carrying numbers around with us. Before then, students were known as apprentices and they spent time embedded in their discipline learning its skills. They either learnt great skills or they didn't; now they get an 85, a 78, a 66, or a 45. Now all modern institutions think in numbers and our social status is quantified by such numbers, or grades, that allow us into other specialized zones – such as the members clubs, the elite institutions, or even into the 'good credit' rating books. The organic nature and capacity of a person has been stripped down to the quantifiable, and this measures the worth of an individual according to such grades. These associated numbers then follow the person around for the rest of their lives, influencing their careers, associations, and social freedoms. Society is now painting-by-numbers.

The mesmerizing void that is modern life tries to appease us with simulated pleasures. Through our unsouling from the greater transcendent wilderness we have become all too easily appeased by seeking inadequate answers to life's meaning. By not seeking for the essential, we cannot hope to be anything other than temporary.

Within the past century millions of people in developed parts of the world have distanced and divorced themselves from nature. We are negotiating how to adapt to a world structured within an increasingly artificial environment. The mutational shift is well underway, and new arrangements will need to be sought.

A potential lack of understanding can disconnect us from a world that is at the same time becoming increasingly connected. For thousands of years our ancestors lived alongside natural forces, learning from environmental cycles, and reading the world around them. This uncoupling from the wilderness is not only in favor of urban settings but eventually artificially constructed settings that will soon be made 'smart.' The profusion of what are called 'mega-cities' are set to implement 'smart' technologies which will be a combination of connected information and communication infrastructures.

A Moment of Reflection

We are, it is said, the most highly-developed and articulate species on planet Earth, and yet we live in a world of reflections. We are doomed never to be able to see directly our own faces. Our face, as well as our 'true face' as they say, is non-visible to us; and so we are guided by reflections and their appearances.

There is a short-story from Argentinean writer Jorge Luis Borges entitled 'Fauna of Mirrors' that tells of a time during the reign of the Yellow Emperor when the world of mirrors and the world of men were not, like today, cut off from one another.[1] Both kingdoms lived in harmony and each could come and go through the mirrors. Yet one night the mirror people invaded the earth and a mighty battle ensued until finally the magic arts of the Yellow Emperor prevailed. The mirror people were pushed back and imprisoned into their mirrors, and

[1] See his short-story collection *The Book of Imaginary Beings.*

punished by being forced to repeat, as if in a dream, all the actions of the world of men. They were stripped of their power and their forms and reduced to mere reflections. A day will come, however, when the magic spell will be broken and little by little these reflections will awaken and will slowly differ from us. Then they will stop imitating the world of humans and eventually they will break through the glass once again to enter the earth.

They say that life imitates art far more than art imitates life. Upon reflection, every culture and society claim a portion of our private psyche as its own. With the narrowing of our sensibilities comes not only a much-diminished reality but also a contracted perspective whereby this condensed form of perception and visibility becomes as hyperreality to us. If it's true that modern life has muffled the call of transcendental mystery, then it is equally true that it has made transcendence both a more needed and yet more difficult promise. The cry for the 'death of the soul' and the unsouling from the wilderness has helped to pave the slippery path toward a simplified hyperreality that is now stealing the show. Fasten seatbelts...

A Bardo Chat with: Aranyani, Hindu Goddess of the Forests

Author (A): Hello Aranyani. Are you there?

Aranyani (Ai): (short pause) Hello…hello!

A: Hello Aranyani. How are you today?

Ai: Today? Why today? I don't have days like you do.

A: Ah yes, sorry. I was thinking in my own terms of time. It's a frequent trap!

Ai: That's okay, we understand. Traps are there to break out of. I am good, thank you. I am well.

A: That is good to hear. I am glad to know you are well amidst all this disconnection going on right now.

Ai: Disconnection? I am gently strolling through my forests. There is no disconnection (another short pause). All is well here.

A: Sorry, I should have been more specific. I meant disconnection between us, humans, and the natural world. It seems that we've done a terrible job of respecting Nature and our environment.

Ai: Mmm, yes, that is so. I am not fond of strolling too near to your civilizations. But why do you call it a job? You see, already you show a wrong way to look at things. Your way of words shows how your mind thinks. Looking after the natural world, as you put it, is not a 'job.' It is a recognition of respect, or mutual interdependence, and of compassion and love.

A: Sorry again. I know that I use my words too loosely. It is the way we use phrases here.

Ai: Yes, I know how your species is. For one thing, you don't listen at all very well. You consider yourselves as a separate species. My dear, nothing is separate. You see space between bodies and you label this as separation. You think and behave like children, and Nature is your forgiving mother.

A: I know, we've got a lot of things back-to-front. Would you care to explain more on this relationship?

Ai: (a soft sigh) Maybe a little. Everything communicates here, it always has. You don't necessarily need a mouth or words or letters to communicate. It all communicates energetically, and you humans are also attuned to this. Every part was supposed to work together. You are strange in that you forgot how to properly listen. And now you build devices outside of yourselves to wrap around the earth – but you don't need them. And there will be a time when you shall know this, and learn to communicate correctly, as you were always meant to – and not with your machine things. All of nature is alive, don't you know that?

A: Yes, some of us do; but not enough, unfortunately.

Ai: You knew better before, a long time ago.

A: Yes, I have a feeling we did. Yet we now need to learn how to know in a different way.

Ai: Well….. (long pause)

A: Hello, are you there Aranyani?

Ai: Oh yes, sorry, I was dancing. I have a tune in my head. It's been given to me from the trees.

A: Wonderful! I was saying that we need to learn how to know in a different way.

Ai: That's not really how it is. Learning, knowing, and all these things – it's all head stuff. You live too much in your heads. You always think you need to grab onto something – to know better, and the like. I would say you have to open up more, and to remember everything that was placed inside you. You are coming to a different place now...

A: Yes, thank you. And what do you mean by 'coming to a different place'?

Ai: I mean you are not in your little tribal units anymore. You are now all over the earth. You grew and connected as you should, and now you are coming to a time when you can really be of help to the earth.

A: You mean as a global species?

Ai: (laughs) You and your fancy words. Yes, you are connecting more strongly with the body of Gaia now. Soon you will find your minds being changed for you. That should be fun!

A: Ah, and what do you mean by that?

Ai: (hums to herself) I don't feel I should reveal too much just now. Not too many of you have realized that your minds are attuned to Gaia, your planet consciousness. Consciousness is not only those thoughts in your head, silly! (laughs). This is the true language, the natural language, and it is everywhere. This language flows through the trees, the plants, the animals, and through all of Gaia. There is a language that connects, and the humans are disconnected from this. Yes, that is the true disconnection. You talk about disconnect from Nature, but really it is disconnection from your shared language. You speak in tongues but only babble silly words.

A: Yes, true - we do babble a lot.

Ai: Babble, babble, yes you do! Like that story you tell yourselves. You call it the Tower of Babel, right?

A: Yes, that's true. And it's a perfect analogy. We tried to build a tower to our Creator and we ended up being divided in languages through our ignorance.

Ai: Yes, that's it right there. You were disconnected through your ignorance.

A: Mm...yes (sighs)

Ai: Don't worry, dear. You still have it all inside of you. Your connection to Origin and the universal language is still there. And you are not disconnected from us either. You are always with us, and you always have been.

A: Okay, sure. And thanks. But by being with you always are we not making the balance of Nature worse?

Ai: Oh, dear ones - it's always about you, isn't it!? Let me tell you that Nature is far more capable of taking care of herself than you are. Things change, yes. And you are making a mess and not clearing up your mess, like children. This is true too. Yet so many more things come to pass that are not in your hands - that is Nature. She is so far beyond your comprehension of her. You think of these separate things within Nature, like the trees and the forests, and the rivers. But you cannot yet see them as being all together as a wondrous Being. She is a Being far beyond your little minds. And she cares for you. Little children, wake up!

A: Yes, yes.

Ai: Be more joyful and love the things you have, and which surround you. The disconnection you speak of is less from Nature and more from yourselves (starts to sing)

A: That is so true – thank you.

Ai: I have to go now…byeee (voice fades into distance)

A: Yes, thank you Aranyani – bye!

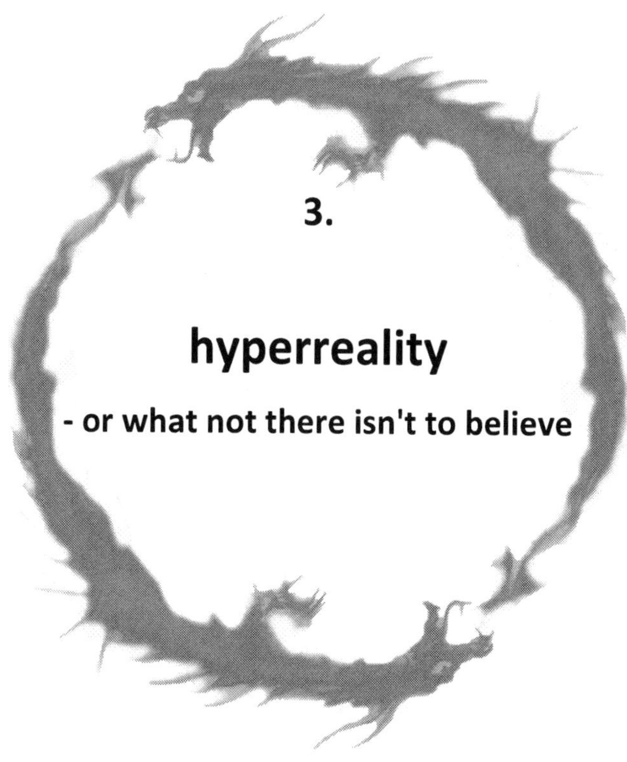

3.

hyperreality

- or what not there isn't to believe

3. hyperreality – or what not there isn't to believe?

hʌɪpə/
adjective
informal

hyperactive or unusually energetic.

'And what then would you do…if you were the ruler of the world for one day?'
'I suppose I would have no choice but to abolish reality!'
'I would like to know how you would set about it!'

Robert Musil

'The attraction of the void is irresistible.'

Jean Baudrillard

If you feel like you are unsure of what is real and what is unreal then you are not alone. Our materialistic mode of life is accelerating and expanding so rapidly that it is saturating our modern cultures to the point of abstraction. Life in materially-privileged societies is increasingly shifting into a world of image, show, and hypernormalization. How to live is being simplified by our media and the further this goes the more we will feel a sense of detachment; as if drifting in an open space that needs to be filled.[1]

People are having experiences, or experiencing events, without actually gaining the experience. It is like dipping into oily water which then runs off without leaving any traces. It feels as if we are increasingly facing an absence. The extreme of this is creating a world where humans feel they are excluded. Many people today are living within their bubbles that are customized by all the digital conveniences tailored to individual needs. By being surrounded by conveniences that satisfy all our needs we are deliberately excluding so much else, including all of life's serendipities. We have unsouled ourselves from the wild things in life in return for safe environments.

---

[1] Or, as a friend once said, it's like a walrus adrift on a sheet of ice.

Reality - whatever that is or was - has retreated behind a spectacle of make-believe that is playing at being the new, shimmering façade for the 21st century. One result of this is that things which once stood in opposition to one another are losing their meaning and becoming indistinguishable. That is, fixed identities that used to make life easy for us – us/them, friend/enemy, good/bad, and the rest – are now more like false realities. Life has shifted, or has been pushed, into a realm of invention that is being exploited ever more overtly by politicians, mainstream media, and their propaganda machinery. Out of this, a different sense of reality has emerged that succeeds in absorbing differences and contradictions and making them seem smooth rather than jagged. And the result is what I refer to as hyperreality.

The hyperreality pill

It is no longer the jagged pill we are forced to swallow, but the smooth pill we are willing to pop. And this smoothness is presented as succulent and easy to swallow. Our modern cultures want us to think that they are simple, smooth, and therefore require our willing obedience. As a consequence, many of us no longer know, or care in knowing, where the resistance is. And if we do feel the need to express resistance, we find ourselves at a loss of where it should be placed. The 'smooth ideal' is that society is managed so there can be no efficient resistance against it. This is what Herbert Marcuse once referred to as a 'comfortable, smooth, reasonable, democratic unfreedom.' The hyperreal evades any real contact. It is like being at the end of a phone call when trying to get through to speak to someone about the awful service we are receiving. We are left either on hold or forced to press through a labyrinth of numbers as the automated system narrows down our choices. Only after an almost unlimited patience, and luck, are we put through to some bland, culture-less voice in an overseas call centre whom we know in our hearts does not deserve the blame or our anger. This evasive strategy of the hyperreal has succeeded in obscuring any site of resistance. It's all so 'real,' and yet of course it is not.

And so, as a remedy to our lack of sites of resistance, we are provided ample sites of entertainment instead. The English writer Aldous Huxley wrote that 'In Brave New World non-stop distractions of the most fascinating nature...are deliberately used as instruments of policy, for the purpose of preventing people from paying too much attention to the realities of their social and political situation.'[1] Huxley feared that people would be rendered passive through access to a plentiful supply of entertainment, consumerism, and a multitude of intoxications. The original notion of hyperreality (a term borrowed from semiotics and postmodern theory) is an inability of consciousness to distinguish reality from a simulation of reality, especially in technologically advanced societies. We are no longer faced with the threat of struggling with our shadows – we are now faced with the threat of our clones. This may be the radical illusion we are slipping into.

Yet the radical illusion of the world has been faced by all cultures. It has been described by mystics, symbolized by art, and struggled over by philosophers. The notion of illusion is not the main issue – rather, it is the medium through which it is conveyed. Or, more importantly, whether it is deliberately exaggerated and amplified. And how, by who – and why? Illusion is now perhaps our greatest industry, especially in western societies. Illusion is the consensus story we are told when growing up and which we all believe in. It's the story that's always been told because 'that's the way it's always been.' No wonder there is so much confusion, which is then fed by another great western industry – therapy.

Hyperreality plays a somewhat different game, with new rules and a different deck of cards. The paradox today is that those of us caught up in the game have no idea what the gameplay is. The problem is that many of these rules are their rules – they tell us that spectacles are to be believed (see Chapter 7); we have enemies to fear (see Chapter 9); and that order and control really equals convenience (see Chapter 10). It seems likely that what the new game is really about is a win-win for the few and compliance for everyone else. Another way to consider this is that we don't have all the cards of the game because they've been stolen by the system. This is similar to a Jorge Luis Borges short story 'The Lottery in Babylon' where all activities in life are governed by the lottery; that is, by chance. And the lottery is run by 'The Company,' the rules of which not only are the rules of the game but become the rules of life. If that's not confusing enough, then we need another hyperreality pill.

Please sir, can I have some more hyperreality?

Hyperreality - the inability to distinguish the real from simulation - has become our new reality structure (perception set) and is constructed so that everyone believes in it and goes along with it. There is an underlying feeling that something is not quite right, yet our sense of reality often appears so extreme that it becomes 'extra-plausible' (again, the notion of hypernormalization). It appears that strange walls of falsehood are being erected between the individual and what is real. The result is a distortion of how we see things. In other words, a perception distortion. To put it simply, hyperreality can be described as the normalization of delusion. When mass society adheres to a collective delusion we call it normal, or 'reality,' and if one person strays too far from this consensus thinking then we often label them as delusional, or unstable. Hyperreality also reflects a flight away from reality, where digital and virtual worlds constitute a substitution. It is as if we have been struck by on-coming car headlights and we are like dazed rabbits in the middle of the road. Better not sit around too long wagging our fluffy tails!

The hyperreal smoothes and soothes all contradictions. When once we thought we had 'left' politics and 'right' politics, these distinctions are now nullified. There is no more any 'left' or 'right,' only agendas that use varying means to acquire the same power. Any basis of truth has slipped into the sleek substitution – the simulation. Let me ask a question: Do we really think that the face of politics, for example, represents any vestige of truth? There is no more truth in politics than there is in someone wearing a laboratory coat in a television commercial trying to persuade us to buy a particular brand of detergent. There is persuasion and falsity that parades as an element of truth, yet it is a pure simulation. We have slipped into an age where the new 'reality principle' tells us that nothing is out of reach and that almost everything can be bought for a price. The real is solid and exists as the flow of goods, services, desires, wants, pleasures, and an almost instant availability.

The question now is how far can the world go before yielding to a permanent state of hyperreality? Perhaps we are already in this state right now; after all, the hyperreal is contagious, like a chain reaction. This thought alone is unnerving. Luckily for me I can step out into my garden to calm my nerves. I can examine my fruit trees, look after my plants and vegetables, do some weeding or cut the grass. The online world stops at the front door when I go out into the greenery of the garden. Yet despite this pleasure I also know that I am a part of a connected world, and that I also require, and need, this connectivity. Both are necessary and important, and so I must keep my head. In the famous words of Rudyard Kipling in his poem

If: 'If you can keep your head when all about you/ Are losing theirs and blaming it on you...If you can talk with crowds and keep your virtue...Yours is the Earth and everything that's in it.'

In the hyperreal world the space of communications is condensed into the simultaneous now; marginal spaces on the periphery are now the hidden spaces where secrecy flows in offshore networks. Our networks of mobility and movement are fragmented into those that privilege some and exclude the many. Even the space above our heads is colonized by the satellites that spy on us. We have street views being watched and analyzed by Google. Our movement, speech, and text being spied on, processed, and interpreted by intelligent algorithms. We have injected a 'smart-virus' into the Earth in order to monitor all activity.

Our smooth digital flows allow - with precision and efficiency - for many aspects of our national and private economies to be shifted to the periphery where the secret networks operate. Only the hyperreal economies remain in the spotlight. There is now a global offshore world that moves in exclusive, mostly secretive networks. The phenomenon of offshoring has transformed peripheral and marginal places into central nodes. Offshored economies had mostly operated in the unseen shadows until the recent scandal of the Panama Papers. The Panama Papers were leaked in 2015 by an anonymous source and listed 11.5 million documents that detailed financial and attorney–client information for more than 214,488 offshore entities. The documents belonged to the Panamanian law firm Mossack Fonseca, which had been operating for decades in establishing offshore accounts and offshore shell companies for wealthy customers. Or, as they often prefer to be called, 'high net-worth individuals.' This massive leaking of documents led to political and celebrity scandals across the world, forcing many politicians to resign from their coveted positions. Presidents are now further pressed to release their tax returns to prove their legitimacy. Yet with the farce within the hyperreal, such players as US President Donald Trump can evade these processes with blatant deceptions. Offshored secrecy and surveillance are central to the functioning of contemporary societies.

Hyperreality is also about disappearance.

Please sir, can you tell me where I can find some hyperreality?

Hyperreality is not only about speed and velocity; it is also about size - things are condensing into ever smaller spaces before disappearing altogether. Our urban habitats, information flows, financial transactions, have all shown increased density at the same time as velocity. Financial crashes today are more explosive because they affect so many more systems on a global level. They are dense in their complexity.

At the core of the condensed form what we once knew as the real begins to disappear. At the extremity of economics, the value of money disappears. It is fiat; that is, only worth what we collectively agree it is worth. On its own it has no value, it is just binary digits swapped between computer screens and fractured into loans. At the extremity of warfare there is no real humanity, only insanity and immense sorrow, loss, and pain. At the extremity of sexuality there is no warmth only the pornography of lust and the commodity of desire. At the extremity of goodness there is the greed to do good. And even at the extremity of love there is no real love, but obsession and possession. Within these extremities we lose touch with anything that once came close to the real. We are in the slipstream of the hyperreal where the substitute replaces its former host. And the substitute is 'always-on' 24/7.

An 'always-on' hyperreal world also creates the illusion of mobility. Precisely because we can be connected throughout the world by the technologies in our pocket we are no longer required to move. We can be in the office while speaking with colleagues across the globe; or chatting with friends on another continent whilst remaining seated on our sofas. The contradiction here is that hypermobility creates its own sedentary life. This was explored in the sci-fi film Surrogates (2009) where people purchase remote-controlled humanoid robots to conduct their social life and affairs whilst the real person remains at home wired to their chair. Of course, everyone chooses a pretty or handsome humanoid to represent them (just like avatars in the online world) whilst their real bodies lie fat and underused in the unmoving chair.

The mobile lifestyle of an always-on hyperreal world appears to promote nomadism. Yet a nomad is someone who doesn't feel at home anywhere, hence their continual need to keep moving on. A nomad is rather someone who is excluded from a settled social life; a person who feels ostracized and excluded from everywhere. Whilst there are mass exiles and migrations happening across the world, this exodus is being undertaken by those people least mobile or least privileged with mobility. We are led to believe there is increased open movement in the world when in actual fact much movement is often out-of-sight and involving ever more elaborate forms of illegality, secrecy, and suffering. Borders are regularly created, policed and surveilled. Those people privileged with social mobility are more likely to be rendered into sedentary lives through the illusion of mobility that is part of the simulation of a hyperreal world.

We have yet little cultural experience to protect us from the invasion of simulation, artificiality, and the hyperreal. It has all happened too quickly for us and our senses have not fully adjusted. Some of us are struggling with aching bodies, restless sleep cycles, and tired eyes from all the screens in our lives. It is not motion sickness we are suffering from more and more but monitor sickness. One of the features of hyperreality is that communication occurs extremely rapidly, and we are bombarded with information almost constantly. As discussed in Chapter 6, much of this information is part of the illusion, only further adding to the sense of the hyperreal.

The hyperreal brings to the fore a convincing collection of

disastrous non-events. Everything that is happening somehow gets reported, transmitted, and commented upon, creating an explosive babble of micro-impacts that dominate our superficial conversations. Then the next day they have disappeared into a black hole of amnesia and replaced by another twenty-four-hour dose of attention-topics. This hyperreal lifestyle creates a background noise; a seemingly endless low static buzz that infests our everyday spaces. It's like the static we experience when changing radio channels, or when a digital television channel isn't yet synchronized.

The bardo years inhabit a world that is living with the consequences of not yet being in synch – and it is a high-velocity, always-connected, post-historic world. For many people who are not yet attuned to this it is highly unpleasant. Things seemingly take place, but we are not quite sure. This is the dilemma. The hyperreal takes the wounded soul and Photoshops it into a caricature of its former self. It becomes glorified and falsely beautified into the less real, but with hyper-appeal. Events and issues are glossed over, making truths little more than quick sound-bites that flash before our eyes. Despite these absurdities we are still living in a world that is physically very real.

The hyperreal in overreaction and overload

We ultra-react because we are continually under bombardment by a stream of information that keeps us in overload. We wish to know as much as possible about what is going on in our environment because this used to be an evolutionary survival strategy for our ancestors. Yet our distant ancestors didn't have the Internet, smartphones, and a whole array of connected gadgets – they had clubs and hatchets. We've changed our rhythms, or rather our new technologically-pervasive environment has altered our rhythms, and we've not had sufficient time biologically, as well as psychologically, to adjust. This is why these bardo times are so unstable. The ground is literally moving beneath our feet. We are waking up to a world in a new rhythm, with a new, faster speed and an altered resonance; and frankly for most of us it makes us feel as if we're partially inebriated. The world is making our children respond to its hyperreal energy, and then subsequently we go about tranquilizing them. Social historian Yuval Noah Harari notes that, 'In 2011, 3.5 million American children were taking medications for ADHD (attention deficit hyperactivity disorder). In the UK the number rose from 92,000 in 1997 to 786,000 in 2012.'[2] In such a world it becomes much harder to practice and maintain certain types of attention, such as contemplative, reflective, and introspective thought. We are accessing information, yet less so are we translating this information into rich, interior states or memories.

It is as if we are afraid to be bored. We may feel that being bored – or being boring – is a failure; that we have failed to make use of all the information and opportunities at our fingertips. Yet the brain is continually working hard to process all information and external impacts, and so we need to take time off to relax, recharge, and replenish. We need to retain our attentiveness instead of giving in to the lazy approach of digitally-offloading our attention. We cannot navigate our own path through life by GPS. At the same time, retaining attention should not require artificial, chemical inducers. Nor should it require copious amounts of fantasy masquerading as the real. Many highly developed cultures are already basking in the 'Disneyfication' effect where western commercial pursuits, practices, and values are promoted around the world as a panacea for all. Disneyfication gives us bigger, faster, and better entertainment that's the same the world over - US mass culture values on the global stage. Disneyfication hides the 'real' places, yet paradoxically many people seem to prefer being in the imaginary. Perhaps its real function is to make us believe that the rest of society is imaginary and only that which resides within the walls of Disney is real. In the hyperreal the spectacle becomes the lived space of our social lives. Disney is colonizing our lives and that colonization becomes the new world map.

The Argentinean writer Jorge Luis Borges famously wrote of a great Empire that created a map that was so detailed it was as large as the Empire itself. The actual map grew and decayed as the Empire itself conquered or lost territory. When the Empire finally crumbled, all that remained was the map. This 'imaginary map' finally became the only remaining reality of the great Empire: a simulation of the once physical reality that has now been colonized by its own spectacle. This is where the Real loses its center and becomes origin-less.

The hyperreal too evades a sense of origin, which accounts for the rise in nostalgia, retro-revival, and people dressing up as superheroes. Star trek conventions, speaking Klingon, and entering a whole new universe meshes with the online worlds and their avatars. In the realm of the hyperreal the origin is origin-less, and real place is place-less. We are given new maps of celebration and celebrity that hide a commodity fetishism - yet where is the meaning? We crave for meaning.

The hyperreal incorporates everything within itself. There is no outer or inner within its realm. The only escape is a form of transcendence - a process or act of gnosis – that can see through the superficiality of the spectacle. This is the current dilemma - our systems are extending but not transcending themselves. Many of us are in this situation: we go for more of the same, only a little bit different. The answer lies in becoming beyond difference. Life has always been a sequence of events that we ascribe meaning too. When we experience this sequence in a reasonable enough form then we create our meanings. It is when this sequence of events and signs becomes asymmetrical, non-linear, or accelerated beyond our limits of standardized perception that we begin to lose our ability to ascribe significance to it. Hyperreality is the zone where this slippage occurs and meaning loses its anchorage. The result is that we feel we are being carried away from ourselves. We are being pulled into the flux and flow of this hyperreality and we lose sight of the ground. Not only the grounded-ness of place, but also our inner ground – that part of us which makes us feel human. It is the soulful part of us that we are losing.

In these 'bardo times' we need to find a new balance and arrangement between things. Our old arrangements are shifting, and those things once in perceived stability and order are losing their moorings. We should remember that the 'Real' exists somewhere inside of us, and keep this in mind as the world outside continues its head-long rush into a frenetic, whirlwind of chaotic events. In the end, we can only truly rely on our own good sense and intuition. As Václev Havel stated in one of his addresses, 'Transcendence is the only real alternative to extinction.'

We must try to remain stable and as sane as possible as life accelerates into its own hyperreality. Otherwise we may not find our own center within the global sensorium of high-velocity living. The ride has only just begun...

A Bardo Chat with: Sia, Egyptian God of Perception

Author (A): Hello Sia

Sia (S): Hey.

A: Thanks for showing up – much appreciated.

S: No worries. We're always around anyway, in one form or another. Anything on your mind?

A: Yes, I was thinking about how life is right now – as I always am! And I was thinking that life is quite a ride at the moment – don't you think?

S: What do you mean?

A: Well, it just seems as if we've entered upon some kind of reality rollercoaster in recent years. And it's not clear if anyone is in control of the program.

S: Nice analogy; but aren't you over-reacting?

A: That's just it – everything seems to be in over-reaction mode right now. Is this how things are meant to be?

S: Mm, yeah. I see what you mean. Of course, it's very much a matter of perception too.

A: I had a feeling you might say that.

S: Then you were right. But I was going to say it all the same. I say it as it's true. Perception is everything. When you can see the truth clearly then the choices become obvious.

A: And is it possible to see the truth, as you say?

S: Possible, but not easy. Truths are one of the first casualties in your reality. I believe you have a saying; something like the first casualty of war is truth? Well, that's quite apt.

A: Yes, we do. And, ironically, that is a truth. We can also say nowadays that the first casualty of news is truth! Yet why do you say it's apt?

S: I say that because in some ways you are involved in a war right now – a war for which type of reality you will collectively share as a species. Your reality has always been based upon how you see it, naturally. I'm not saying anything new by telling you that you exist within a perception-based reality. The question is how you choose to perceive, and this can be a matter of self-training or of external influences. This is the battle that has always been waged. Historically this was easier as mythologies were readily accepted by the masses. In your times now, it appears that there is a lot more confusion over which stories are more believed and accepted. Or perhaps I shouldn't call them stories, as this word has too light a meaning for you. Maybe we should stick with belief systems and social narratives. Perceptions are being manipulated in your times to a very high degree. It is confusing many of you.

A: Tell me about it! It feels more and more as if we are in a form of hyperreality where the distinction between what is real and what is false is blurred. Is that not so?

S: I'm inclined to agree, for the moment. No reality at your level is ever fixed. We may refer to them as sub-realities for now. Since you are shifting through Ages, from one stage of your civilization to another, there is a great amount of flux and disturbance. There is also a great amount of energy coming in and playing a degree of havoc with life on your planet at the moment.

A: A great amount of energy? That sounds ominous.

S: (gentle laugh). Well, it depends on your perception and perspective, of course. I don't really know how you would define 'ominous.' In your human form you tend to see all things as either one or the other. Nuances are not your strong point. Anyway, perhaps I should talk about this energy a little?

A: Yes, please do.

S: Okay. The energy is necessary for where things are going. In what may appear paradoxical to you, from your perspective, this energy is both disruptive and stabilizing.

A: Yes, I've heard something similar to this. But could you clarify more?

S: Yes, I will clarify. Imagine you pull the plug out of your bath in order to release the bathwater. There is a build-up of energy around your plughole as all the water attempts to get released. This build-up creates what seems like a vortex around the hole, no?

A: Yes, I know what you mean.

S: Well, this vortex is a stabilizing form that serves to hold the pressure of the water, the energy, whilst it finds release and moves on to another form, or another use. Similarly, there is a great amount of energy upon your planet right now that is being used to assist the transformation between Ages. It is both disruptive as well as being similar to a vortex and holding the energy. This formation of energy across your planet has the effect of seeming to accelerate events, such as time. This acceleration you have already alluded to as what you call 'hyperreality.'

A: Ah, I think I understand now. And so, this hyperreality phase will pass once the old energy has been released - out of the bath, so to speak - and a new energy has entered.

S: Correct. From your perspective this form of hyperreality is an existing and real phenomenon. Yet from my perception it is a brief moment within a larger span of time, which is necessary for the forward momentum of life and development upon your planet. Perception gives us a distinction between seeing something as a chaotic, rushing energy; or as a dynamic but stable concentration of energy. Your reality structures are trying to accommodate these energetic fluxes.

A: Thank you, Sia; that's helped a lot. And do you think our reality structures will also shift?

S: Of course. Reality structures is perhaps not the best term to use here. Again, I find myself limited by a constrictive vocabulary. By structures I mean arrangements. A reality - your reality - is an arrangement. These are energetic arrangements that correspond to different scales of perception. What you are able to perceive right now from your planetary perspective is quite dense. Your planet's vibration, and hence your reality, operates upon a lower plane. This will change as events pass. New forms and arrangements will come into being in accordance with different energetic correspondences. Am I making sense?

A: Yes, please go on.

S: Only to say that all forms of reality are in movement and are all-inclusive.

A: All inclusive?

S: Yes. You participate within them. You are within the

bubble as it moves and shifts, so to say.

A: And can we ever see out of this 'reality bubble'?

S: Well, yes. This has been the objective of many of your wisdom paths for centuries. There are many traditions that teach and train for this. But that is another story. You also have images and renditions of this in your creative arts.

A: Well do?

S: (laughs). Yes, you do. But you will have to look for them. That's your homework – if you want it!

A: Yes, I know. You cannot give us everything on a plate.

S: Certainly not. Where would the learning be? Where would the fun be?

A: Indeed. So instead of going down the rabbit hole, to quote a popular phrase, we are going down the vortex of a plughole?

S: (pause). I'm not sure I totally resonate with that phrase. But I think I receive the general meaning inherent within it. You do use odd phraseology at times. It is awkward, but also somewhat amusing.

A: I'm sure it is!

S: Well, I wished to say that you are moving through what you may refer to as an energized vortex. And this will affect the nature of your sensory perceptions, although more so in the long term. Think of it all as a journey of discovery, and nothing is static.

A: I think it was an ancient Greek philosopher who said that All is flux.

S: Maybe. Although many systems of Greek learning came through from the Egyptian schools. But that is another story, as you say. Well, that's it for now.

A: Thank you, Sia.

S: No problem. And don't forget to hold on - you will get through it! Bye.

A: Bye.

Endnotes

1 Cited in Urry, John. 2016. What is the Future? Cambridge: Polity Press, 29.

2 Harari, Yuval Noah. 2017. Homo Deus - A Brief History of Tomorrow. London: Vintage, 45.

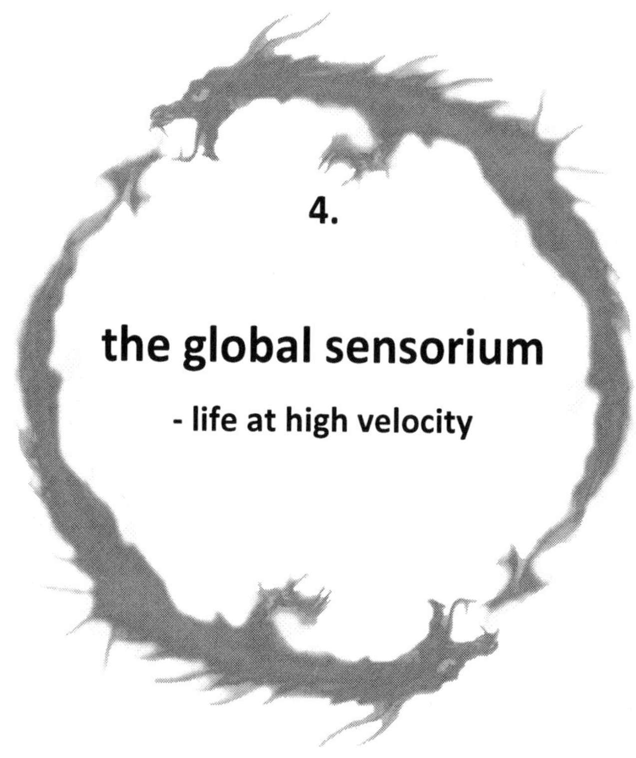

4.

the global sensorium

- life at high velocity

4. the global sensorium – life at high velocity

sɛnˈsɔːrɪəm/

noun

the sensory apparatus or faculties considered as a whole.

The only solution now is to move constantly or flee definitively.

Paul Virilio, The Administration of Fear

Our sense of reality is now constituted from a pervasive array of technological structures. And we are not going back–there is no reverse mechanism. Let's ask a question: who would wish to go back to a time when there were no mobile phones? We would have to make appointments by the fixed landline in our homes and offices and once we left them there would be no other way to communicate.

Remember all those times of running late for a meeting; or perhaps for a date with a potential partner? The sweat, the anxiety, the desperate talking to oneself that all would be okay and that they would still be there waiting for us when we arrived late because they had faith in us. And now? Now we sit back shifting through our emails or playing a new app on our phones, and we text *willBL8 – wait4me*.

Some commentators have argued that there has been no new major technological advance in the last half a century. For me, this represents a failure of vision and perspective. The older technologies were massive inventions such as the telegraph, telephone, radar, and television. These were single instruments or systems that spearheaded a revolution. Yet the age of the 'single device' is over – today is the age of swarming, connecting, linking, where a myriad of technological innovations, upgrades, and adaptations are rushing in from all sides. Technology is becoming less about the hardware and more about the software that connects everything together. Technological advances will be measured less and less by the bulk and more in the operating software systems and ethereal strings of code. And this all coming together will usher in monumental socio-technological change.

Life for many of us has entered a period of uninterrupted time which gives us the sense of speed and acceleration. Events are already moving so fast that it's hard to keep up with the news on the latest innovations, technological research, discoveries, and the rest. Too many things are happening all over the place at such a rapid pace. No one person has all the information or is able to connect all the dots together in order to see where all this is going. It's just too much, and it's scattered all over the globe. It 'should' all come together at some point; yet until we reach that moment we are swimming in unprecedented change and movement. Time is literally being reorganized, and instead of opposing longer working hours people are now embroiled in an all time-consuming availability. Accelerated time is also about how many more hours we have made ourselves available. We don't leave the office behind at six o'clock when we go home. In an accelerated world we seldom have the luxury of leaving things behind. More and more it is about living in the elongated ever-present. We can imagine this as living in a domed global sensate city called the 'Global Sensorium.'

The global sensorium is obsessed with the instant.

The instant is both the future and the now; or rather, both are merged into one instant. We are living the future by being present. Perhaps that is why many people cannot find anything to look forward to because there appears to be no forward beyond the present instant. Human civilization has entered a period of intensified life that many of us experience as being high-velocity, highly connected, and information dense. We are now living in a kinetic reality that is increasing its spin of velocity. We are measuring in milliseconds rather than seconds.

If space-faring travelers were to visit our modern lives they would probably conclude that we were in a primitive technological stage of worshipping *instantaneism*. We are wanting to live in the omnipresent as if we can now become the all-seeing, all-knowing participants of a new world happening in 'real-time.'

Welcome to the Now of 'Real-Time'

Modern life has pushed us to the point where we are obsessed by real-time, on-time, and the everything-now. And this is especially the case for life in urban-dense environments. Delay must always be avoided (eradicated!) as if it were a dangerous virus. In fact, we can buy insurance to compensate us if we are subjected to the experience of unnecessary delay. Waiting for the slow webpage to download threatens our well-being. The previous state of 'real time' that our parents experienced now delivers to us a sense of inertia. This real time of our parents is equated with the euphemistic term of 'quality time' which means being with the family, spending time in the garden, or strolling aimlessly through shopping malls. It used to signify that a time or an event was real, such as a music concert or a sport event. We would make travel arrangements to arrive at the event venue; we would wait in queue to enter; find our seats; and then count down the minutes in anticipation for the event to begin. This was real time and it involved the unfolding of time in a very real sense.

Real time as we once knew it now takes on a different meaning and represents the slow time that exists as two separate words. Whereas the 'real-time' of today is so instant it requires to be written as a hyphenated word in order to distinguish it from the 'real' real time of yesteryear. Real-time is linguistically entwined and cannot be a space apart – it is happening too fast to be written as two separate words. Real-time now means having the event streamed into our lives – into our device or our living room – at the exact moment it is happening without us having to be there. We are synchronized with it by being simultaneously afar. This is the real of real-time now: the immediate download, the simultaneous streaming that needs no waiting. We can access it whilst on the move, on public transport or annoyingly in a restaurant with friends.

Real-time is not equitable – it favors the favored. High speed and high velocity are almost always rolled out to the privileged first. And the favored are those deemed worthy to have the right of access. Real-time, if you want it now, is an access economy. If you pay for it, then you get it streamed to your account.

What, no account? Then you're not with us; you must be in some under-developed, over-colonized place. But if you stream without paying then we'll get you like we got Kim Dotcom.

Time as we once knew it as a measurement is becoming obsolete. Our quantum sciences tell us that we are all simultaneously connected at a fundamental field level; that is, we are always 'there' as well as 'here.' Our spinning atoms may be both inseparable and light years apart at the same time. In our reality we are thus both connected and separated at the same moment. We are secretly connected and yet we rarely truly communicate. Where is the sense of 'time' in this?

Likewise, the stars we see in the night sky exist only thousands and thousands upon thousands of years in the past; it is only their irradiated light that now reaches our senses. When we observe the stars, we are participating in the 'real time' of our past. Many stars may no longer exist, already undergone super-nova deaths in their suicidal stellar explosions. Time is a measurement of velocity that sustains a consensual illusion. And we are bound by this illusion. Nothing is 'real' in itself but only in relation to other unreal things.

Will the invasion of real-time be the death of introspection? Will the new generations involve themselves in reflection and retrospection? Many of our children are being encouraged to train in techniques of accelerated speed reading – to read faster and comprehend more – to save hours of time. Publishers of books for children are now selling box-sets of 'Accelerated Readers' for young schoolchildren. An online promotion on Amazon claims that 'Thousands of schools across the UK use the Accelerated Readers programme to boost

Children's Literacy levels and love Reading.' Books are available with such titles as *Accelerated Learning Techniques for Students: Learn More in Less Time*, and *Accelerated Learning in Accelerated Times*. And, fortunately for the eager reader, they are 'available for immediate download' so you don't even have to wait for the next-day delivery. Waiting is now almost considered as something negative; as if waiting is a barrier to achieving what we want rather than preparing us for something we can gain from. And then there's the speed of information.

Information without meaning is, after all, only a jumble of letters or digits. Information is rapidly accumulating yet it's still not clear whether it is adding to meaning or not. Supercomputers are now operating in petaflops, which is way, way faster than flip-flops. As of June 2016, when the 47th edition of the TOP500 list of the world's top supercomputers was released, the world's number one ranked supercomputer was China's 'Sunway TaihuLight' with ninety-three petaflops per second. But wait a minute (a whole minute?!) – what's a petaflop? Well, a petaflop is equal to one thousand million million (10^{15}) operations per second. That is, a thousand trillion operations per second. In other words, it is equal to quadrillion calculations per second. So that means that our supercomputer here can perform a record-busting ninety-three quadrillion calculations per second. Hold on - what does *that* mean? No really, what does it mean when the human mind is incapable of comprehending such speeds. It makes no human or humane sense.

There is so much going on now that it is as if we have entered an echo chamber full of bouncing data, information, voices, and thoughts; and we cannot tell where they are all coming from. All we can manage to get hold of are the traces these speeding data sounds leave behind. Or perhaps *we* have become the traces - each one of us, speaking into our devices and leaving a part of ourselves in our social media posts. We are like a multitude of fractal data-bites for archiving in some cloud (and that's not a real cloud, by the way).

Fractal Places

French philosopher Paul Virilio believes that we have now entered the *acceleration of reality*. He says that in the current era we have reached the limits of instantaneity, the limits of human thought and time. Also, that this era of accelerated reality has led now not to the end of history, as some have wanted us to believe, but to the end of geography.[1] Virilio says we have polluted our measurement and sense of distance and place, and within this there is a loss of body; a loss of the corporeal. Time, place, and space have become fractalized. That is, our historical sense of continuum, of physical expanse, is being eroded and broken-up into fractals. We need to stop this fractalization of reality, says Virilio – but how? Places are now becoming less important than the connections that serve them. It is the interconnecting flows that create the status, the significance, rather than the static physical location. Hubs are only as important as the places to which they connect to and the flows which they facilitate. In this case some of the busiest airports in the world are those that offer the best connections rather than final destinations.

According to current statistics, the third busiest international airport is in Dubai. Yet Dubai has very little final traffic, apart from business people and the few excitable shopping tourists. And the busiest international airport in the world is in the United States. This may not

---

1 A reference here to Francis Fukuyama's treatise The End of History

surprise anybody; yet it isn't JFK (New York), or O'Hare (Chicago), or Los Angeles; it is Hartsfield-Jackson Airport. That's right; Hartsfield-Jackson International Airport has been the world's busiest airport consecutively since the year 2000, with currently around 105 million annual passengers. And where is this airport? It is in Atlanta, Georgia. Exactly, it is in Georgia. Are roughly 105 million people visiting Georgia annually? I doubt it. Yet Georgia is a hub airport – it deals in connections, with transit flows. It is not a place but a place-connector. In the high-velocity world of the global sensorium it is not the place that is the attractor; it is the flows, the endless possibility for continued movement. Likewise, it is no longer the light that attracts the human eye (or the moth), but the lightning – the *blitzkrieg*.

We're now in *Blitzkrieg*

War is the sad and unfortunate example of this *blitzkrieg* (lightning war) strategy. It is an accelerated hit hard and fast tactic, so they don't see it coming. This military policy has now transferred into so many other areas of our modern lives; from economics, education, entertainment, security/policing (drones), video gaming, communications, and inevitably social relations. Time is now a culprit in our global sensorium: we are living under the dome of high-velocity everything.

This strategy has especially infiltrated into global trading and taken it beyond human grasp. Blitzkrieg high-frequency 'flash trading' is now rampant within the world's global stock exchanges as turbo-capitalism takes our finances into orbit. This military terminology is apt as the technologies now used in the financial markets are as powerful as those used in military defense. It is no surprise either that the military and the financial sector are now the biggest funders of research into artificial intelligence. Together these sectors seek to exploit the ever-faster realms where no human mind can reach. It was in the early 1980s when global stock exchanges were first connected in what was real-time back then; this connection was called 'Program Trading.' Ever since then the global financial markets have operated at ever faster speeds, and in increasingly unmanageable ways when viewed from a human perspective. And then algorithmic trading was introduced, leading to high-frequency 'flash' trading practices on computers that are as sophisticated as those used at the highest defense levels. Next to come on the scene is AI financial trading.[2]

The majority of financial trading has no time context that either you or I would be familiar with. It is too quick to be humanly shared, and thus exists beyond the capacity for human cognition – it is beyond our senses and operates in a hyperreal realm. It is no longer in the hands of operators; competition is no longer negotiated, it is flash traded before we can blink.[3] Yet all is not smooth as the markets also contain their own fears (and their trader's fears) in what they have dubbed 'the fear index' – the Market Volatility Index (MVI). It appears that instantaneity, high-frequency flash trading and algorithmic trading in the markets induces its own fears - no need to invent more. Stock markets worldwide can plummet in seconds causing widespread panic. Everyone trembles at the possibility of impending loss, not knowing from where it will come next. The only thing we can be sure of is that it will come again. Will it be from one of the over-ambitious 'flash boys'? Or from a Ponzi scheme revelation? Perhaps it will come from the slip of a human finger or the acerbated act of an algorithm?

Yet we can rest relieved knowing there are now

[2] For more information, see The Economic Singularity by Calum Chace.

[3] For more information, see Flash Boys by Michael Lewis.

circuit breakers in place to supposedly block such sudden stock plummets; but one wonders whether all (loop)holes are covered. Where one hole closes another one can just as quickly open up. Just like my dog; as soon as I block one hole in the fence he soon finds another one to escape through. It makes me think that everything – yes, everything – is just a bunch of holes somehow sown together to look solid. But no, all atoms are solid...aren't they? All matter is as thick as a brick, isn't it? Sure it is - as long as you don't read up on the latest science. Maybe it's best to think that the world is still flat, and Bigfoots live in the center of the Earth. But the holes...just don't think about the holes. And don't think about the figures either.

Unfortunately, the figures can be wrong; algorithms and their mathematics are only a program after all. Benoit Mandelbrot claimed, in 2004, that the conventional mathematical models used by the stock market 'are not only wrong; they are dangerously wrong.'[1] Furthermore, computerized program trading does the deals behind peoples' backs, and only flashes back a few reports for stock market screens. In short, algorithmic economies are beyond our comprehension. Time is too slow for artificial algorithmic 'intelligence,' which is now conducting its very own insider trading. Previously, insider trading and financial scams were conducted in chronological time – in hours and days – by human perpetrators who could be named and shamed in media trials. Now the economy has been taken 'out of time' – beyond chronology – and into a blur. Yet algorithms cannot be taken to court and jailed, so everything's alright – right?

Banks and economic institutions move so swiftly (no pun intended) that there is literally little or no time – or place – for accountability and integrity.[4] After all, how can accountability be identified when accounts are either offshored or moved too quickly to be traced? And neither do the global figures add up. Almost all of the world economy is now 'financialised' in that 'by 2010 the total annual value of foreign currency transactions was US$955 trillion - more than fifteen times the value of world GDP at a mere US$63 trillion.'[2] It is also said that 70 per cent of all US stock-market trading takes place via computer-aided high-frequency trading. That is, through algorithmic trading. Accelerated algorithmic trading takes finances away from the 'real economy' and towards a less stable and less governable 'casino capitalism.' As an example,

[4] The SWIFT code is used to identify banks and financial institutions internationally. They are used in bank transfers, especially international transfers.

after economic deregulation huge derivatives were created which caused derivative contracts to grow tenfold reaching a colossal US$500 trillion, many times greater than global GDP. Similarly, by 2006 the assets of British banks were ten times the size of Britain's GDP and resulted in a huge rise in systemic risk. Credit[5] loses, bailouts, quantitative easing, national debt – what are the figures, and what does it all mean?

Economies, and hence debt, now run into the trillions, and yet these numbers have no possible physical reality to them. They are illusionary digits that by fiat (consensual decree) bind and control our global affairs, as well as making and breaking (i.e., devastatingly ruining) individuals, groups, corporations, and nations. Yet it seems there is no getting away from this incumbent system as all markets are now interconnected. Like airports, it is their interconnections that matter more than their location. To be 'in' the market you need to be 'of' the market, which means being one of their connections, and going with the flows of their rules and regulations. Otherwise your connection is cut – economic death.

Likewise, in order not to face being cut out of the connections, modern life is increasing its always-on

---

[5] See the book Offshoring (2014) by John Urry

connections and flows. And it seems that things are becoming somewhat congested.

Are we at Saturation Point?

Modern western culture is taking itself to a saturation point, and with accelerating velocity. It is possible that this high-velocity is required in order to trigger a necessary tipping point that will initiate the next phase. Similar to how an airplane needs to achieve a certain degree of high-velocity acceleration on the runway in order to initiate take off. Of course, the question that then needs to be asked is – what will come *after* saturation?

There is already a high degree of psychic stress bubbling up within modern life; much of this coming from the velocity of dis/mis-information arriving at full throttle. Connectivity is cool, no doubt about that, but now the global world has arrived on our doorstep bringing new risks, new obligations, and unprecedented circumstances. Naturally, people are feeling overwhelmed.

With hyperreality also comes hyper-vision, as if we cannot have one without the other. This enlarged 'hyper' view provides us with an excess of visibility; an abundance of nervous system stimulation that can feel very unsettling. We now have to be aware of those people who are hyper-sensitive or display hyper-sensitivity to impacts. Dr. Elaine Aron in the film *Sensitive: The Movie* tells us that 1.4 billion people are highly sensitive.[6] The array of complexities, uncertainties, and disruptive events that increasingly make up modern life are providing an abundance of nervous energy. We may not know how to measure this – yet many of us are *feeling* this.

In a world of constant updates we are always behind on catching-up. Life is being lived more and more through our inboxes, our social media messages, our online profiles, listings, and through our own obsessive personal updates. We are racing against ourselves within a high-velocity, hyperreal environment to be always catching-up. And the pace quickens and begs us on. The result is that a new form of wealth has been created. Whereas wealth has traditionally been defined through financial acquisition and consumption, the 'new wealth' is now measured in freedom from or the power over time, availability, connection, and movement. A measure of our wealth is also the power we possess over our own mental time. Welcome to the global sensorium – a whole sensory

---

[6] For more information, see http://sensitivethemovie.com/

apparatus, brimming full of emotional stimuli, connections and flows, time-constriction and, for some, senses overload. As Virilio declares – 'I prefer the revelation to the revolution.'[3]

Velocity Revelation

Time has revealed itself to be simultaneously running away and running the show. We have our clocks, our watches, and an increasing array of digital devices that manage time automatically. We no longer have to think about switching between the seasonal differences to save daylight as our devices do this for us. When we chat online with friends or colleagues across the world we often forget (or prefer not to remember) that their time zone is different. It doesn't matter that they are in their pajamas as the only time to talk is now, in real-time. And if this means one unlucky person (probably in the minority time-zone) getting out of bed then so be it. Time no longer gives us a fixed location with an excuse. Time is that *flux-zone* that makes us available as it rushes away from us. We only get the briefest of opportunities to say whether we are available or not – and even this choice is sometimes taken away from us by the automated decisions of our devices.

And through this we are being *delocalized*. Yet this delocalization occurs in many ways. It may be through a loss of fixed available time; a loss of fixed work space; or being in the position where we are unable to say 'no' to inconvenient requests. In fact, inconvenience is no longer a possibility. Sedentary life is being gnawed away at until it becomes a mausoleum.

New modes of imagination and innovation, as well as a whole new range of impacts, are affecting our senses. As a species we are trying to adapt – to re-wire our senses - yet we are faced with a velocity of change that can feel overwhelming and gives us the impression that we cannot keep up or re-wire in time. This high velocity is affecting, and changing, how we think about and experience cause and effect. Our understanding of linearity is becoming fuzzed in the turbulence of accelerating events. Maybe it's time to W8 up B4 its 2lte, as the modern parlance now goes.

As an ex-university teacher I have been unfortunate enough, on more than one occasion, to receive emails from students using this condensed form of text-speak. It was as if the student couldn't find the time to type in full letters, or maybe their minds were in text-twitter mode and their fingers numbly complied. Likewise, videos and audio talks are more and more chopped up into sound-bites to make them palatable for a generation on-the-go. Then again, I'm not sure that watching a long video on a tiny phone screen would be either ideal or healthy anyway. Sound bites are ideally suited to the size of the devices which transmit them. Images are quickly consumed and then forwarded, shared through Whatsapp, Messenger, Instagram, Snapchat, and the rest, and so on, ad infinitum etc – you get the picture. It's an incredibly fast movement of the image. They speed around the world as if inside a social Hadron Collider. Our data – bits of binary code - are traveling almost at the speed of light and smashing into each other as if replicating their own version of the Big Bang. And everything is sealed into this high-velocity perspective of reality. The global sensorium is all-inclusive and all-consuming. The whole hyperreality is packaged and sealed in its shiny wrapper, and only the genuine mystic knows where the exit door is. There is a door, of this I am sure, and it has been available at all times and in all cultures. Yet it is a door that is invisible through its own visibility – hardly anyone is genuinely looking for it. Until then, the Bardo of waking life continues.

Seeking Inertia

In the face of rapid acceleration and high velocity there is a compelling need to find a state of inertia that is a state not of apathy but conscious inactivity. Conscious inertia is a counteraction against excessive acceleration and the exhaustion of velocity. It is learning how to 'freeze' ourselves – to create *frozen moments* – amidst the rush of our modern high-frequency lives. Time really is one of our rarest commodities, and as such it must be saved from a social execution. It may be necessary for us to try to develop these 'frozen moments' as a way to step back from our high-velocity lives.

In an earlier book I examined ways for psychologically retaining balance within a world of constant distraction. As the global sensorium expands it will become ever-more necessary to detach from situations that are distracting, noisy, or confusing. In a high-velocity world it is necessary that we make sure our energies are not sucked away from us. It is about making choices not to allow the external impacts to affect us, or to enter into our private inner space. Sometimes the global sensorium needs to be kept at bay.

It's not about leaving the world behind either: we still need to be relatively alert in case some online stranger from the African continent wishes to use our bank account to transfer huge amounts of money to their dying mother. It is about being attentive to the fast-moving world of information, discussion, emotions, and the rest. It is not only about creating a physical withdrawal but also, perhaps more significantly, creating a mental and emotional private space of inertia. Or, to use modern terminology, it is about unplugging from the global sensorium.

Life in the global sensorium is about exercising patience and restraint under the right conditions if we want to better find balance in such a high-stimulus environment.[7] The alternative may be that we unconsciously get sucked into a high-frequency 24/7 info-entertainment Disneyfied world more akin to *The Matrix* on acid. Maybe we need to take time out from the tablet, the posting of photos on social media, or scrolling through the endless messages on Facebook that are increasingly interspersed with customized advertising. Life in the global sensorium is as much about knowing when to let go of things that cling to us. There is an old story about this that I relate here in a modern telling:

---

[7] See Breaking the Spell (2013)

A River to Cross

One particularly fine spring day two men of faith were out taking a good long walk through the hills and ravines close to their retreat. The elder of the two was a well-respected man of piety and morality who had served his community for many years. The younger man regarded the elder as his mentor and role-model. The two men were also good friends and often enjoyed their company together. On this occasion, as on many others, the two friends were sharing stories and articles of their faith.

Later that morning, during the course of their walk together, they came upon a shallow river that blocked their path. It was then that they noticed, under a tree by the side of the river, a young, attractive woman with her head in her hands. Upon seeing the two men approach the young woman sprang to her feet in obvious relief and pleaded with them to help her across the river.

'The water is shallow, this I know,' said the young woman notably distraught. 'Yet I have a terrible fear of water from an unpleasant experience I had as a young child. Please, you must help me across – it is imperative I reach my destination across the other side by lunchtime.' The young man listened to her pleas yet was moved not. Instead he eyed the young woman, her scantily clad attire and her suspicious demeanor.

'For my part, I cannot' said the young man, 'for it is unseemly for a man of my faith to be in close contact with such...such a one as you. You must walk across the river by yourself.' The young man proceeded to wade across the shallow river as the young woman wept. The young man, proud in his adherence to discipline, expected the older man to follow him across the river. Yet when he looked behind he saw, to his horror and disbelief, the old man shamelessly pick up the young lady and carry her in his arms. The young woman, in fear of the water, pressed her body close to the old man and clung to him tightly. When the old man had reached the other side he carefully put the woman down and, without another word, continued on his way.

The young man, stammering, soon marched off close behind him. The young man did not know what to say, so shocked had he been by what he saw. He walked alongside the older man in silence yet inside he was fuming. He had respected and looked up to the elder man for so many years. He had considered him his mentor, a role model in piety. Had he, after all these years, been wrong in his respect for this man? Was he just a fake? A false man of faith? A hypocrite? The young man was tormented by these thoughts and yet he did not know how to approach the older man - how to break this news to him?

At noontime the older man sat under a tree and spread out a small picnic he had prepared and offered it to share. The young man ate in silence, his inner world in turmoil and gripped by doubt. After lunch the two men continued their walk in silence and by dusk they had returned to their retreat. As the older man was about to say goodnight and retire for the evening he turned to his younger friend and said, 'You have been wishing to speak with me on a certain matter all day and yet have kept silent. Now is the time to speak – I am listening.'

The young man poured out his grievances and his disbelief at the older man's actions. It was, he said, an act against the cleanliness of their faith, to be in

> intimate contact with such...such a woman of her calling. When the younger man had finally finished his outburst, the older man turned to him calmly and said, in a steady voice:
>
> 'I picked up that woman and carried her to the other side of the river. And then I put her down. But you, you are still carrying her!'

Sometimes, as the popular phrase goes, we are our own worst enemies. Being connected allows us access to a whole gamut of information, news, false news, gossip, celebrity culture, and virtually the whole world stage. There seems to be no greater time than the present to be in control of our senses at a time of senses overload. Or maybe it's preferable to dive right into this modern hoax of a simulated reality that's ready to seduce us all. If so, let the hoax begin.

A Bardo Chat with: Chronos, Greek God of Time

Author (A): Hello Chronos. Are you there?

Chronos (C): Greetings. I am here.

A: Thank you. First of all, I would like to say that I know there is some confusion over your identity, as you often seem to get mixed up with Kronos, the Titan father of Zeus. Yet you are an actual god of time, right?

C: (sighs). Ah, there are some things which time does not seem able to correct, and that confusion is one of them. It really is best if we don't go there right now. For your purposes, I am a god of time - at least in terms of time and perspective that your species is familiar with. If I say any more on this, it will only confuse you further.

A: Okay, thank you Chronos. Apologies if I have caused any confusion over this.

C: No worries – no time lost (low chuckle).

A: In that case you're the very person – sorry, god – that I need to speak with. I'd really like to get a handle on this time issue we seem to be experiencing here on earth.

C: Would you care to elaborate?

A: Sure. It seems that the human experience of time is speeding up, accelerating, and this is not just my own sensation. Peoples from all over are saying similar things. It just seems as if a day is no longer sufficient to do all the things we once used to do. And yet our devices that measure time record no objective difference. Is there something actually happening here, or is this just a collective delusion?

C: Collective delusions are something your species is very good at. However, in this case there is indeed more to it. It is interesting that you mention time as both a measurement and as a sensation, an experience. And it is both. There is no physical property of time in terms of your devices, such as the watches you put on your arms. Your days are cut into segments through your devices. The objective sense of time comes from celestial movements. These you have measured over aeons through your calendars.

A: And so we have both artificial time as we have created and a more objective time?

C: Yes, if you wish to place them into two simple categories. On your planet throughout history you have created measurements of time that you adopted. You chose calendars to suit your needs, to measure your ages and your cycles. Some of these were aligned with grander cosmic cycles by those people who had knowledge. Yet many of your measurements and calendars were either developed or continued by people who had no knowledge themselves. So these time devices, if you wish to call them that, became 'out of time.'

A: And we also changed our calendars to suit various religious movements.

C: That is so. In this context, time became a structure to regulate your social development.

A: And we still have that today in terms of social management. I mean, in how our work routines are calculated, and when we 'clock on' and 'clock off' for work. Time is a monitoring tool in this context.

C: That is so. This is lower level use of movement. As I said, there are movements that happen in your cosmos which can be aligned with to better understand what you would refer to as 'time flow.'

A: The flow of time?

C: Yes. This flow has presence in your reality. It can be used as an indication. Everything, as you know, is in a state of flux.

A: And our calendars also may in fact be in a state of change?

C: Not only the calendars themselves but the phenomenon which they seek to measure. Your planet does not exist in a vacuum, despite what many of your kind like to think. It has a place, and role, in a much grander scheme. And this grander cosmological scheme involves movements and changes on such a huge scale that it is beyond your understanding. However, there are effects, or rather phenomenon, from these cosmological changes. These effects can be measured by those calendars that are correctly aligned with geophysical processes. The geophysical state of your planet is similarly aligned, or rather corresponds, to cosmic phenomena. But the important point is in the experience. Energetic variations that enter your interstellar and then solar neighborhood affect certain astronomical constants.

A: So, wait a minute. You are saying that larger changes or movements in the cosmos affect the planet Earth?

C: Precisely. This has always been the case. As you people like to say – this is not rocket science.

A: And that these changes may bring with them energetic affects?

C: Yes, both in energetic shifts as well as alterations in astronomical constants. Together these phenomena influence the spin of your planet and thus its energetic environment which nurtures you. You thus have geophysical impacts as well as those that affect your human nervous system. These you generally refer to as physiological and emotional impacts, or disturbances. These impacts do much more than just affect your durations, your time frequencies. They are responsible for behavioral features across your planet. Yet this is another subject. Let us stay within time, for now. Generally, you have so far been unable to measure these changes because you have yet to produce the appropriate instrumentation.

A: Yet we are feeling these changes, aren't we?

C: Indeed, you are. You could say that you are going to war over them. You are experiencing, or sensing, specific cosmological impacts that are, and always have been, influencing life and development upon your planet. These are natural occurrences. You are sensing a different quality to that which you know of as time. Yet your instruments have not picked up on this in any consistent manner (chuckles).

A: Wow.

C: The more sophisticated your technologies become, the more they will find these energetic behaviors. You are already investigating what your science calls the quantum field. As you probe further. Well, I should say, as your consciousness and understanding develops you will discover patterns in this time field. I call it 'time field' although this is very vague term and not altogether correct. I use it in conjunction with your vocabulary and image sense. Forgive the inaccuracies. These are not good for a god of time! (low laugh).

A: No, sure, it's fine – I understand. So, tell me, will these energetic impacts create a disturbance in our reality.

C: They already are and have been for some time. You often experience them through other means.

A: Such as?

C: Such as geophysical disturbances like earthquakes, eruptions, and various environmental manifestations. In your social environments through warfare, revolutions, and other cultural upheavals.

A: Oh dear...

C: Don't worry too much about this. Your species is actually hard-wired to be adaptable to these changes. My suggestion to you now is that you remain grounded and stable. The last thing you need to be doing in these times is, as I believe you say, going off the rails?

A: Yes, that's right! It sure does seem like now is the perfect time to be grounded and in control of our emotions. I didn't think the subject of time would have all these associations.

I started out asking about time and our calendars and we've ended up talking about earthquakes, war, and revolutions. And these are all time?

C: (laughs). Well, there is no real clear-cut thing called time, if the truth be told.

A: But you're the god of time, are you not?

C: I am. But that is the denomination you people gave to me. Again, it is a simplification in order to represent more complex issues. It might be easier to say that I – and all of us here – represent certain phenomena rather than singular features. Time is a good example. It is not one thing. It is rather a phenomenon that binds and corresponds. It is integrative. Time is not one thing. As your scientists say, it is a relative thing.

A: Yes, but could you give an example?

C: Yes. You notice that your human bodies grow and then decay with the passing of this time called time.

A: Sure. It's one of our greatest burdens!

C: Mm, well. Your body grows old, as you say, and yet you do not sense a similar passage in your sense of inner self. This inner you is not affected by this passage of time. Yet the world around you changes alongside you but in so many different ways. Your 'time' affects how you perceive and interact with the world around you. Yet this is different for everybody. You notice things in your house start to change, or decay. Or some things even grow healthier, such as the trees in your garden. Everything has its processes, and yet you relate to them according to your sense of time. And this is completely relative. It is, to put it bluntly, how you choose to live with it.

A: So, what you are saying then is that no one can experience my time for me. It is only for me. We are all children of time.

C: Exactly!

A: Thanks, Chronos, that's been a great help. I've enjoyed our time!

C: You're welcome. As I always say – any time!

Endnotes

1 Cited in Virilio, Paul. 2012. The Great Accelerator. Cambridge: Polity Press, 80

2 Urry, John. 2014. Offshoring. Cambridge: Polity Press, 64.

3 Virilio, Paul. 2012. The Administration of Fear. Los Angeles, CA: Semiotext(e), 71.

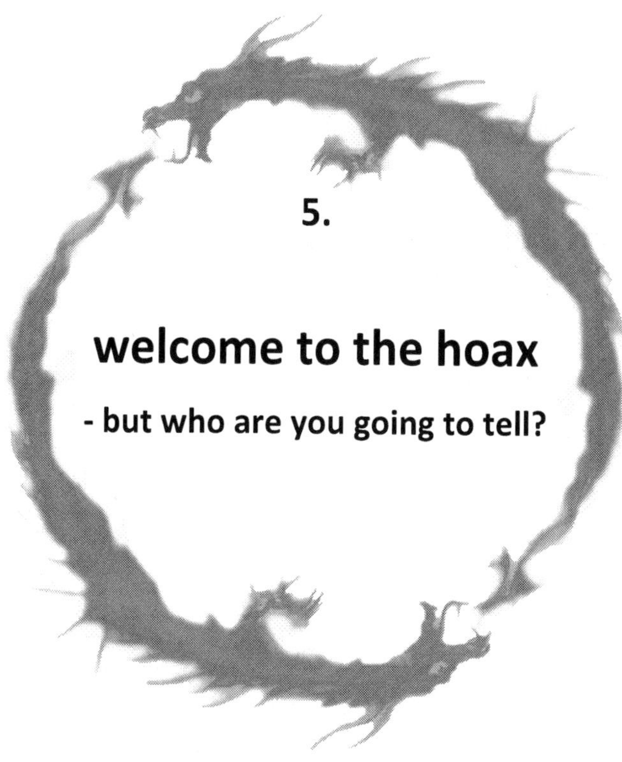

5.

welcome to the hoax

- but who are you going to tell?

5. welcome to the hoax – but who are you going to tell?

hәʊks/

noun
a humorous or malicious deception

verb
trick or deceive (someone)

When a nation becomes unmoored from reality, it retreats into a world of magic.

Chris Hedges, *Empire of Illusion*

Let's be honest here - we do not live within an accurate portrayal of the 'real world.' We assume that our perceptions – our sights, sounds, and textures – are accurate descriptions of the world around us. But they are not; rather, they are the filtered representations that have been processed through us. We can never perceive the world directly, just as we can never look directly into our own faces. The world we perceive 'out there' is a projection of the inputs we have received; it is our brain's best guess based on the data available. And since most people's brains work in a similar manner, the final projection onto life's movie screen is more or less similar. I say more or less, because if anyone has ever read a Philip K. Dick novel, or journeyed with shamans, ingested certain mind-altering substances, experienced deep trance, or undergone deep meditative states, etc, then the reality experienced is somewhat different. The direct perception of the Real, say the mystics, leaves a person with no doubt of the truth of reality – it is complete certainty. The alternative – our general state of perception – is based on an internal simulation that our physical apparatus (our body) has interpreted for us. This means that technically life as we know it is a simulation, or simulacrum – *an image or representation of someone or something.* And I'm not the only person saying this; scientists are also picking up on the notion that reality is only a representation.

Donald D. Hoffman, a professor of cognitive science at the University of California, Irvine, has spent the past three decades studying perception, artificial intelligence, evolutionary game theory and the human brain. And his conclusion? He says that the world presented to us by our perceptions is nothing like reality. According to Professor Hoffman, what we call objective reality is just a collection of points of view. No one, he claims, can measure the same object in the exact same situation and get the same results. Yet this should not surprise us since we've had the theories of quantum mechanics hanging around for the better part of a century now. We've had enough time to get used to the idea that the particles that make up our physical reality have no observer-independent existence. We live in an observer-influenced reality. It's just that most of the time our observations seem to correspond to what we know as life - more or less. As the physicist John Wheeler famously put it, 'Useful as it is under ordinary circumstances to say that the world exists "out there" independent of us, that view can no longer be upheld.'[1] The brain filters out the majority of inputs in order to keep us sane. What it finally passes on to us are nothing short of 'brutal representations' that allow for our general survival.

Let's be practical here – how could we get along with the world if all we perceived were the underlying energetic vibrations? We *need* to live in a 'de-coded world.' Yet where once this de-coding went without being questioned we now realize that it's not so simple anymore. And this is what I call 'The Palimpsest Problem.' A palimpsest refers to a parchment, or piece of writing material, that is used several times, each time the previous information being erased. Rather than throw valuable parchments away our ancestors used to reuse them by erasing the older writing, much like we used to do as kids in our notebooks. However, often traces of the earlier or original writings show through. Remember those instances in spy movies where the secret agent finds a piece of paper that some information has been written on and then scrubbed away? Usually the clever agent will take out a pencil and rub it over the ingrained, erased letters and a message will emerge. This is the palimpsest, where we have information placed layer upon layer of previous rounds of information. And that is exactly what I see happening today.

Our societies, especially modern media-driven cultures, are creating layer upon layer of substituted representations of reality. Sometimes the new layers are over-simplified – *hypernormalized* – in order to portray a basic 'Us vs. Them' world. Yet the result is the same – our sense of reality becomes flooded with these over-layered portrayals and representations. What was once only partially real (our observer-influenced reality) now becomes far-from-real in that our cultures become saturated with superficial content created by our mainstream media, politics, and similar propaganda channels. And this is all part of the simulacrum – the unsatisfactory substitution. Layer upon layer of projected interpretations of what is 'real' thus leads to the 'The Palimpsest Problem.' One way or another, however you look at it, life is a simulation of something, which itself is a simulation of something else. Another way of calling this is the 'soup of the soup,' and here's a story from the exploits of the well-known Nasrudin that explains it:

> A kinsman came to see Nasrudin from the country and brought a duck. Nasrudin was grateful, had the bird cooked and shared it with his guest. Presently another visitor arrived. He was a friend, as he said, 'of the man who gave you the duck'. Nasrudin fed him as well. This happened several times. Nasrudin's home had become like a restaurant for out-of-town visitors. Everyone was a friend at some removes of the original donor of the duck. Finally, Nasrudin was exasperated. One day there was a knock at the door and a stranger appeared. 'I am the friend of the friend of the friend of the man who brought you the duck from the country,' he said. 'Come in,' said Nasrudin. They seated themselves at the table, and Nasrudin asked

> his wife to bring the soup. When the guest tasted it, it seemed to be nothing more than warm water. 'What sort of soup is this?' he asked the Mulla. 'That', said Nasrudin, 'is the soup of the soup of the soup of the duck.'[2]

The highest function of simulation is to make the real disappear, and at the same time to hide the fact of its disappearance. The whole event never happened. This is the true art of the mainstream media, for example, and it is a highly articulated conjuring trick.

Great mystic literature from all over the world has spoken about our reality as being, in some form or other, an illusion – as not *real*. Sure, but some things seem very real to us: we get hurt, endure pain (sometimes horrific, inhumane pain), and we suffer as well as we love and experience joy. Yet we are still told that it is all an illusion in that it is only a copy of a greater truth. As Plato would say, it is a shadow of the original Pure Form. Maybe Shakespeare said it best when he said in *As You Like It*,

> "All the world's a stage,
> And all the men and women merely players;
> They have their exits and their entrances,
> And one man in his time plays many parts.'

And now this illusory play is being taken to its extreme; to its illogical 'logical end.' Welcome to the simulation that has now substituted our modern lives. Welcome to the play of perception. Welcome to the hoax.

A Seductive Hoax

Historian Yuval Noah Harari states that according to mathematics, 'since there is only one real world, whereas the number of potential virtual worlds is infinite, the probability that you happen to inhabit the sole real world is almost zero.'[3] There has already been a lot of talk about whether we are living in a computer simulation. This debate was largely triggered by philosopher Nick Bostrom's original essay 'Are You Living in a Computer Simulation?' (2003).[1] Bostrom famously argued that the evolution of humanity will inevitably lead to a posthuman state in which our descendants will have immense technological power, unless they blow themselves up beforehand. And if they do reach this advanced stage then they will have the technological ability to create complex simulations of their ancestors (that's us!) in which

[1] Nick Bostrom has posted his essay online; see http://www.simulation-argument.com/simulation.html

everything seems real. Even the consciousness of the 'characters' in the simulation will feel as real. These posthuman descendants will be able to create as many simulations as they wish – which leads us to the scientific theory of multiple dimensions. And if they will be able to create as many simulated universes as they wish, then they will naturally create far more 'simulated characters' than the number of actual ancestors. Therefore, according to Bostrom, given that the probability of any of us being a simulated character is much greater than that of being a real ancestor, it can be concluded that we almost certainly live in a simulation.

As intriguing as it seems this absorbing philosophical conundrum is not the focus of this book. The issue we face is a closer-to-home cultural phenomenon – the social representation of life that seems more unreal than real. In other words, the cultural allure of a lifestyle that, like the palimpsest, appears to be further from the original 'real' with each retelling. And this sensation of the 'uncertainty of the real' is more exposed, more directly in our faces, as we pass through these bardo times. Simply stated, what's on offer is far more seductive and attractive than ever – and this is the hoax. It is in fact a hoax more insidious than the 'computer simulation' model for at least that model would aim at some internal consistency. What we have is an imitation, and an unsatisfactory one at that.

The social simulacrum is an unsatisfactory imitation or substitute. It attempts to substitute offerings that disguise the genuine, and which perpetuate the illusion that what we see and hear going on in the world is the actual truth. Yet these illusions are like pantomimes, catering to those people attracted to the façade. And this façade has been gradually built up – a process known as 'function creep' – over many years. And it has got to the stage where it can fascinate us and lure us in. Yet since it is a simulacrum, a copy, it naturally must be inferior because all copies are. However, we do not see or perceive this inferiority because we are not meant to. This 'wonderful reality' that is a simulacrum is then spread across the globe in the hope that everyone will want to participate. An analogy here is the brilliant scene in *Hukkleberry Finn* by Mark Twain where he shows how Huckleberry manages to persuade his friends that his painting (whitewashing) of the white fence is not a chore but actually a privilege. His friends then give him gifts in order to take turns painting the fence, and Huckleberry sits back grinning. He has duped them first into thinking that this chore is a wonderful experience; and secondly into desiring, and paying out, to participate. The whitewashing of the fence is our current whitewashing of the real. And the danger here is that not only do we allow this to happen but that we *naturalize* it to ourselves by participating in it.

The all-encompassing Simulacrum

The simulacrum that is now the system is all encompassing. Everything that we know, or think we know, exists within it. And this simulated substitute attempts to contain all anomalies. A reflection of this can be seen at the end of the second Matrix film – *Matrix Reloaded* – where the Architect (a Freud look-alike) says that the matrix was reprogrammed to incorporate all of its anomalies into the new program. That is, even anomalies are needed to keep the program running for they are a part of the program itself. It is a totally inclusive reality-matrix that has no exterior. In the *Matrix* films it is possible to un-plug from the matrix. For us, we have not yet discovered a simple escape route. However, there have always been methods and techniques for transcending *beyond* the simulacrum that surrounds us.

In the terminology of humanistic psychology this

form of transcendence has been called the path of 'self-actualization.' And yet we only get the privilege of 'working on ourselves' when other more primary needs have first been realized. These needs include the physiological needs of food, water, and rest; then the safety needs of shelter and security; following these are the social needs of belonging, love, relationships; and then the esteem needs of accomplishment. Only then when these needs are met are we in the privileged position to consider fulfilling our true potential – self-actualization. And yet the simulacrum of society and culture does a very good job of occupying us with the lower needs throughout our lives so that we hardly ever get the opportunity for any form of self-actualization. The simulacrum is very good at keeping us busy, distracted, and engaged with other things.

Our social systems promote, even unashamedly, those aspects which may appear as the anomalies. Music artists who rage against society - such as singers whose pop-rock songs protest the system - are all massively promoted by the very same system that gets rich from them. Such anomalies are not only tolerated or accepted, they are also actively encouraged. The system seeks to incorporate all genuine alternatives. Everything feeds into the same hoax. The world that we think we know is being represented to us through copy, as a form of radical illusion. Life is then lived and experienced through the new medium of a 'proxy life.' By accepting this we succumb to a life that is lived indirectly as if feeding upon the menu rather than the meal. Our real, genuine, and deep hunger is ignored. Of course, there is suffering, conflict, hatred, and all the rest, that is all very real to us. Yet what we rarely stop to consider is that *we* have made all this real through our own stories – through those narratives fed to us by society. Our cultural palimpsests are stories built upon stories.

Whether we wear a turban, sport a long beard, shave our heads, or dress in particular types of clothing, we are indicating to those whom we meet that we adhere to a particular narrative. When people are willing to die to go to paradise; to kill to bring glory and honor; or to destroy lives for a few bank digits – they are all adhering to their stories. And stories only have value if there is a common consensus. It is exactly the same with money, whether it is fiat currency or hard metals; they have a certain value because there is a consensus story around them. Yet what good is a bar of gold if you're dying of thirst in some desert and the only camel driver with water does not accept your gold?

Our social stories have formed structures of meaning which have validity within a similar network of stories. Once we encounter another social structure of stories that do not tally with ours then we usually end up going to war with them. Each story we tell ourselves is mutually reinforced within our own network, confirming its validity, until we end up believing what everyone else around us believes. And the great hoax is that each simulacrum uses language, images, and social rituals and reinforcements specifically to create completely new realities. If we wish to understand our future then the best thing we can do is to decode our cultural stories. We literally live within a world of fiction. And in a world of fictions and stories, reality will always lose out. Reality, or the real, has always been forced to fit our stories of the world – and always will. Whether we are told the world is flat; that the earth is the center of the solar system; or that we will go to hell if we are bad. The simulacrum of stories will always force reality out of the picture. We live within a sea of stories, and these are the simulated programs.

It is crucial to understand how the simulacrum programs us so that one generation does not 'unknowingly' submit to programming the incoming generation. Otherwise the system becomes a continual programming machine. And the hoax knows how to sell itself over and over again, using different catchphrases for different generations. In terms of popular culture its banality is often dressed up and sold off as the fascinating, the intoxicating, the entertaining, the alluring, the game-play, the fun, and all the rest. But banality, whatever it is dressed up as, is still banal underneath its sheen. And for those of us in modern cultures especially we are lured into accepting the banal just as the naked emperor wears his non-clothes. It's the fast food of meaning. We take our portion, feel nourished and refreshed, and then walk away seemingly satiated only to feel hunger pains again shortly afterwards. It does not truly fill us with anything of substance. And this is the banality of the hoax: we are not given anything of genuine meaning or worth. But so many of us fall for it. Really, let's ask ourselves – how many of us are truly happy?

We may wonder why so many people in highly-developed cultures are so depressed. According to a recent report published by the *Journal of the American Medical Association* (JAMA) 16.7 percent of 242 million U.S. adults reported filling one or more prescriptions for psychiatric anti-depressant drugs in 2013.[2] This is one in every six people and is an increase from 13 percent in 2012. Despite the simulacrum of happiness, there is an overwhelming amount of anxiety and depression. And not only within the general populace either as this syndrome is endemic also amongst the 'stars' of the show. Many of our well-known celebrities are in therapy, or have been in therapy, or are in dire need of therapy; for ailments ranging from alcohol and drug abuse, failed relationships, stress, and other factors. Only the most gossip-driven stories are splashed over the show-time news; yet deep under the surface many celebrities silently suffer and are already addicted to popping their pills. In the last few years alone we have seen 'famous stars' drop down like drugged flies, including Michael Jackson, Heath Ledger, Philip Seymour Hoffman, and Prince. Just pop in 'famous stars died of drugs' in your online search engine as I have just done and see what comes out. In fact, you might even need to narrow down the search as there is far too much information. Why not write – 'famous stars died of prescription drugs.' The greatest show on earth it seems is underwritten by a medicinal diet of therapy and pills.

---

[2] For more information, see http://jamanetwork.com/journals/jamainternalmedicine/article-abstract/2592697

There's no escaping parody. The escape itself would only be a caricature.

It seems that nothing anymore can be taken at face value, if ever it could. Simulated environments attempt to erase any competing ideas or ideologies that may contest them; or else they seek to incorporate them. They whitewash over any opposition, re-pixelate the screen so that everything looks in accord. Yet they do this not only by eradicating opposition but also by creating a false sense of opposites, dualisms, and opponents. Everything, from our sense of choice, our politics, our economics, is manufactured and packaged for us, just like prescription drugs. What we are facing more and more has less to do with the real and more to do with its replacement – its replicant.

The Rise of the Replicants

We pride ourselves on knowing the difference between the real and the imaginary. Our sense of reality is guided by signposts called dualities - by the 'right' and 'wrong' and the 'left' and 'right.' And yet these home-spun superficial structures are overused as substitutes. They are like replicant signs that distract us from what may be going on below. We are presented with a packaged 'hoax' reality that fakes its oppositions and its choices. We are asked to make a choice between one thing or another without having any choice in the selection offered to us. There is an incredible sleight-of-hand going on, and this is the illusion of free choice. We think we have free choice when we are asked to choose between A, B, or C – whether they are candidates, objects, policies, etc – when in fact all we are being offered are limited options. To be offered choice is not the same as having free choice, and yet the difference is blurred. When we are given the choice between A and B, the sleight-of-hand is distracting us from the question – 'In what type of system do I live which produces the choices of only A or B?' Also - 'where are all the other possible choices beyond A or B?' Our perspectives are being managed into a specific and controlled focus so that we miss the broader picture. We rave over our stories of the 'left' and the 'right' and we even transfer our stories onto placards and go onto marches. We say that 'we' are labor or conservative; democrat or republican, when in fact what we are really saying is that 'you gave me the option of A or B, and I chose A – and now I'm going to defend my choice.' These are the external dualisms, the false paradoxes that create the illusion of a nuanced playing field. To any keen observer they can be seen for what they are – superficial, paper-thin cut-outs parading as a pantomime.

What are the choices of freedom available to us? In terms of staged politics, what is our 'freedom' of choice when the whole system behind the candidates is beyond our choosing? The illusion of choice distracts us from realizing the very absence and lack of choice that really exists. It is the magician's sleight-of-hand trick that distracts our attention from the object of true value. In this case, the fact that our political systems are stage-managed to exclude choice and to be as limiting as possible for the general populace. This is a simulacrum of freedom that replaces its former representation of repression (whether feudalism, dictatorship or authoritarianism). The special effects are more subtle, smoother, and cause less opposition. Or, in the words of Herbert Marcuse – 'A comfortable, smooth, reasonable, democratic unfreedom prevails in advanced industrial civilization, a token of technical progress.'[4] Marcuse also noted that the 'Free election of masters does not abolish the masters or the slaves.'[5]

Simulation plays with the notion of substitution,

replication, and replacement. Most things are a copy of something else. The real – the original – is out of sight, unseen by the untrained eye. Any semblance of the real has undergone substitution – welcome to the hoax. And so, we may ask - where are the originals today? What *is* even original today? Even our personalities (our personas) are a mask; our identities are socially conditioned sets of cultural identifiers – where is the original 'I'? Who is the original 'You'?

The social-cultural simulacrum loves nothing better than to make a grand performance about so-called 'originals.' For example, even 'original' paintings are copies because they are a copy of something else that was imagined or copied from life and transferred onto the canvas. You cannot say any painting is 'original;' this is just a fake word used to cover up the simulation. What we call an 'original' painting is merely the 'first copy' before the other copies arrived; and then after that the fakes arrived, which is yet another layer to add to the overall deceptive simulacrum. And yet the 'first copies' still fetch incredible amounts of money (money being another object of simulation which is based on perceived or consensus value). Examples of this ridiculous spending spree include the $300 million paid for the painting *Interchange* by

Willem de Kooning in September 2015 (as did Paul Gauguin's *When Will You Marry?* in February of the same year). This overblown behavior ends up looking more like a parody than anything else. These events in our lives are supposed to give us meaning, to provide satisfaction and achievement; and yet they are governed by the artificial, the shallow, and the show. These are events which are ever drifting toward their own vanishing point. The replicants guard the portals to the void.

The simulacrum of contemporary cultures is awash with the synthetic image. Synthetic images go viral because they replicate through our social and technological networks. They replicate without boundaries to be copied, pasted, and passed through social media posts, blogs, inboxes, etc, until they have been reproduced up to millions of times. They are so far from the original they are no longer its ghosts – they are its phantasmagoria; the visual driftwood contributing to the ever-growing flotsam of psycho-candy. Now movies have merged with the synthetic in computer-generation images (CGI) that create a cinematic simulation away from real objects, persons, and settings (see Chapter 7). We are in the process of obliterating the traces of our existence as we slip closer to the void.

Perhaps the trick, if there is one, is to be aware of ourselves within the simulacrum that surrounds us. This degree of self-awareness is similar to what Gnosticism addresses (see Chapter 12). It is up to each of us to be responsible for our own vigilance.

Being Vigilant within the Hoax

Now is a good time to be alert. If there was ever a time to be watchful then the bardo times are certainly one of them. Each day of our lives we are impacted, influenced, and swayed by forces external to us. We are inundated within the simulated environment that is the hoax. And like fishes in water, the nature of our environment is often hidden to us in plain sight. Cultural institutions and social systems spread their conditioning forces over us, ply us with propaganda, and sell us playful images and pursuits that appeal to the collective. It is a representation of reality that prefers its participants to be mechanical, without creative thinking. What we need now is a keen attention; a capacity to see things coming at us from a distance. It is time to take a more active role in our own watchfulness.

As we walk daily through the simulacrum we should take note of our steps. There are always moments, opportunities, when certain choices have to be taken. The simulation (hoax) likes to play out on those choices we make, so each of us should be aware of our choices and decisions. We need to be alert to the nature of the hoax as there's little chance to walk away. We may pretend it's not happening or ignore its charms, yet we have to be 'in the game' in order to exist in our social and cultural environments. The best strategy would be to play the game wide-awake. There is a fine line from being players to pawns. Not being a pawn means being aware of the nature of the game. And it is all made up of stories – both the stories told us and the stories we tell ourselves.

As I stated at the outset, everything is within our own heads. There is nothing 'out there' that is not also within us. If we are hoaxed, then it is because something inside of us allows it to be so. If we are to cross through these bardo times, then we need to know the hoax for what it is – an illusion. As Albert Einstein once said: 'Reality is merely an illusion, albeit a very persistent one.' Welcome to the art of perception management.

A Bardo Chat with: Hermes, Greek God of Travel, Thievery & Trickery

Author (A): Hello there, Hermes. Are you there?

Hermes (H): (shuffling noise) Ahoy there. Hermes is indeed here!

A: Great, I wasn't sure if you'd turn up. I heard you are hard to get hold of.

H: (laughs) Ah, you've been listening to my detractors! I'm always around. You know, I don't think there is ever a still moment.

A: Well, you are the messenger for the gods; and you are the god for travellers and for boundaries. I guess that means you are always on the move.

H: So true, so true. I'm always zipping here or there. There are really no boundaries where I go. And if there are, well, I just cross over all of them! I must confess I don't get these boundaries everyone talks about. All worlds are mixed, whether under or over! (laughs).

A: Actually, that's something I wanted to talk with you about. Our world here is full of boundaries, and many of them are invented. I refer to it as a simulation. Someone, or let's say a nation, comes over and draws a boundary on a map. Then you have a new space. But it's just a story that becomes his-story.

H: Yeah, sure, tell me about it. I see you people doing this all the time! We give you an open, clean slate and then you go drawing all over it, inventing your new rules for each game. You literally take out a pen and then it's line here, line there. You keep changing the lines and then changing the rules. We all thought you were a schizophrenic lot until we came to realize it was an infantile learning process. You expel a lot of energy in these territorial games.

A: Do you think it is all a simulation?

H: What does that really mean? Everything is a simulation in one way or another. A simulation is just something that is a copy or reflection from the Real. So, sure it is. But that doesn't take its validity away. I deal with what you call simulations all the time, and it's real enough for many intelligences. It is what you have made from your slice of reality. You make the simulations within the bigger simulation. It's a kind of trickery really, but it can also take you further away from where you need to be.

A: And I suppose trickery is your game, isn't it? You are Hermes the Trickster, right?

H: (laughs) Sure thing! But all the trickery I do is for a purpose. And much of it has been to help you guys out. Did you know that? I've done lots of trickery but for your well-being. But now many of you are enjoying what you call sleight-of-hand for your own selfish ends. This is not real trickery, sorry to say. It is manipulation, and there are many of you who love this game.

A: And how do you see this type of trickery - this manipulation?

H: Like I said, it's infantile from where we see things. It is more thievery than trickery. Everyone seems to be telling lies to each other, and you are building up a reality that steals the truth away. Every layer of lies that you put out takes your further from your Source. You are putting veils over yourselves and smiling while you do it. It's not clever, whatever you may think.

A: No, not clever at all. Manipulations and lies are never clever. But there are those people who think it is. I think they feel it gives them power.

H: Power, perhaps. Yet power is only a game. And like I said, this game takes you further from yourselves. I think maybe you're getting lost in your own game.

A: That's interesting. Do you think we are also creating borders for ourselves?

H: Without a doubt! In the early days you had Heaven and Hell. Now you have everything in-between too. Borders are made real by your imaginings. Your world exists first in your head; then you make it into something real outside of your heads. Your borders are your power lines. There are no borders from where I'm seeing. I see a bunch of children playing in their schoolyard. You are sitting in your sandpits building fake castles and walls that are soon to fall. If you build with the wrong intention, then such things will never last. And what's more, they will collapse on top of you. You'll be a bunch of children submerged by your sand games!

A: What a thought. What an image!

H: Yes, and here's another thought. I may come again to play some tricks on you! (laughs).

A: Please do. Some fun would be good. One last question – how can we know what is real and what is not?

H: You have to play the game without cheating! As a messenger of the gods I could give you some helping hints, but that would take away from your own achievement. Even the gods have to achieve, you know. You must find that distinction for yourselves. You must discover your own achievements; otherwise, why be human?

A: Yes, indeed – why be human. Thank you, Hermes, for the chat.

H: You're most welcome. Remember to play the game well! Bye.

A: Goodbye.

Endnotes

[1] Amanda Gefter, "The Case Against Reality," https://www.theatlantic.com/science/archive/2016/04/the-illusion-of-reality/479559/, April 25, 2017 – accessed April 28, 2017

[2] Shah, I. 1985. *The Exploits of the Incomparable Mulla Nasrudin*. London: Octagon Press, 107.

[3] Harari, Yuval Noah. 2017. *Homo Deus - A Brief History of Tomorrow*. London: Vintage, 139.

[4] Marcuse, H. 2007/1964. *One-Dimensional Man: Studies in the Ideology of Advanced Industrial Society* Oxford: Routledge, 3.

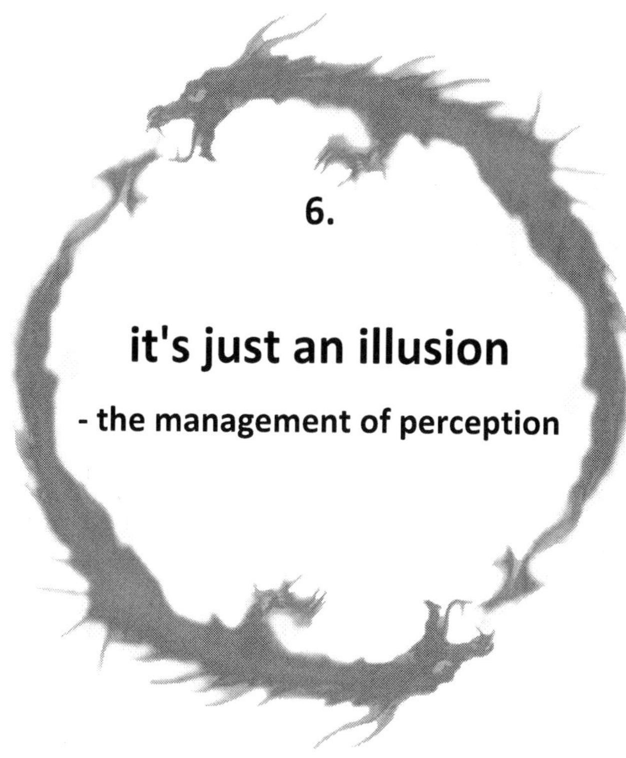

6.

it's just an illusion

- the management of perception

6. it's just an illusion – the management of perception

ɪˈluːʒ(ə)n/

noun

an instance of a wrong or misinterpreted perception of a sensory experience.
a deceptive appearance or impression.

We live in a society in which spurious realities are manufactured by the media, by governments, by big corporations, by religious groups, political groups. I ask, in my writing, 'What is real?' Because unceasingly we are bombarded with pseudo realities manufactured by very sophisticated people using very sophisticated electronic mechanisms.

Philip K. Dick

For the truth is, that life on the face of it is a chaos in which one finds oneself lost. The individual suspects as much but is terrified to encounter this frightening reality face to face, and so attempts to conceal it by drawing a curtain of fantasy over it, behind which he can make believe that everything is clear.

Jose Ortega y Gasset

On the face of it life is a chaos, says Jose Ortega y Gasset; and so, a curtain of fantasy is drawn over this frightening reality. It is too complex, too dirty, too full of uncertainties and unknowns that would only disturb the masses. People, after all, need to be comforted. That's why another reality is conjured up that is manufactured by the media. Philip K. Dick asks what is real as we are under the bombardment and assault of pseudo realities. We may ask ourselves the same question, what is real? Perhaps our perfect crime has been to hide the real so well that our modern societies have ventured beyond the illusion of reality itself. The perfect crime is the perfect cover up. The power to make better choices comes from the power to have information. Information has been the life-blood of our societies and cultures and has been guarded tenaciously throughout the centuries. Whether sacred 'divine' knowledge or information on how to improve one's life in general; they have all been guarded by various institutions throughout our history. From priest kings to shamans; from religious figures to scientists; from life-coaches to gurus; and from governments to mainstream media – information has always come at a price, if it has come at all.

Information was something traditionally given to

people in a controlled manner. The masses were provided information generally in-keeping with their level of intelligence as well as their need to know. And traditionally, both these factors were notoriously kept low. Anthropologists tend to agree that homo sapiens has conquered the globe due to its flexible ability to cooperate on a mass scale and with strangers. And historians add to this by saying that human societies have proved so successful because they are able to socially organize themselves and survive as long as order is maintained. That is, the unified elites have always been able to dominate the disorderly masses. The masses remain disorganized if they lack sufficient access to credible information. And that is where the cult of information and the spectacle of entertainment enter into the picture.

Modern life has become inundated with information, and it has spilled over into the hands of the masses. The age of illiterate masses listening to their local church sermons to receive the word of divine guidance is long gone. The Gutenberg Press managed to signal the end to the monopoly on scribes. Books began to bring new and inspiring information to the masses whom were quickly learning to read. And then something enormously powerful happened at the end of the 20th century – the communication channels were multiplied, and people began to talk back, in droves. People were no longer only receivers of information as in the past; they could now produce the information themselves and share it with a potential audience of millions around the globe. The planetary talking box was opened, and people were finding they had voices. And that is when propaganda stepped up a notch to become even more of a hardcore science and governmental tool.[1]

In our not so distant past, if you wanted to seize political power in a country then normally your first step would be to control the army and the police; that is, the institutions of brute force. Today though it is only in the less 'democratic' countries where dictatorships still use such overt force when trying a coup d'etat. The real war is the war of minds. The day after the fall of Khrushchev in the former Soviet Union the editors of *Pravda, Izvestiia*, and the heads of the radio and television were replaced but the army wasn't called out. More recently, after the failed coup attempt in Turkey, in July 2016, the incumbent government came down heavy on what it considered to be the country's alternative media. In the immediate

---

1 For more information see my previous book The Struggle for your Mind: Conscious Evolution & the Battle to Control How We Think.

aftermath, 148 journalists and media workers were jailed, and 169 media and publishing outlets were closed down under the state of emergency.[2] And that was just the beginning. In any society it is important who controls the news information, and how it is dispersed. Yet since we now live in an 'Internet Age' of global communication and information networks, it is increasingly harder by the day to keep a tight control on things. In a sense, Pandora's Box has already opened. And if there is so much information out there then how do you maintain order? The best answer is – provide more of it. Provide so much information that people are drowning in it. And then add some more to discredit what is already out there. People are then not only swimming in information but begin to drown in it. And the rest – well, that's entertainment!

The Illusion of Truth

Whilst we are trying to stay afloat our mainstream institutions are peddling us a simplified version of events and of the world in order to create a sense of reality suitable for us. It is an attempt to create a sensory bubble

---

[2] For more information, see - https://www.hrw.org/news/2016/12/15/turkey-silencing-media

around us that we are told will make life easier. After all, too many ‘reality events’ would only serve to break down this simplified bubble and give us all a headache. And so, a spectral illusion is created through our mainstream media and news in order to offer a simplified vision of the world to us. It is Us vs. Them; Good vs. Bad; Developed vs. Undeveloped; Legal vs. Illegal; and all the rest of these bland dichotomies that are brandished as deep truths.

We have an ‘official culture’ that functions as the ether. We are immersed in it even if we are not aware, as fish in the sea do not always debate the water. This official culture creates the signs and symbols that affectively dictates our slice of reality: money, credit, status, intellect, policy, major sports, lesser sports, celebrities, good film, bad film, popular book, ignored book, love, sexy, seduction, disappointment, etc, etc. We buy into all these terms so deeply that it is no surprise to learn that we are a cultural species in therapy. We have been brought up and ‘educated’ to protect ourselves with the illusion of truth. Everything withdraws behind its own appearance, so that things appear to take place even when they do not. This is the great absence in our lives - excuses riddled with illusion, hiding through false appearance. We are left to decipher the world, to try and pull back the illusionary curtains. The crime of life is its incompleteness - a living absence that gnaws at us. We drift between second hand news as ghosts drift between walls. If everyone believes in a lie, it doesn't stop it from being a lie, or make it into a truth.

The illusion is often what many people want to hear, rather than the brutalities, or mundane reality, of life. It is a 'people-syndrome' that we wish to see a part of ourselves in those we idolize and worship. It is often a desperate, or unconscious, projection of self-denial. It is as if we prefer bland information and filtered news, or celebrity gossip, as a complement to one's own sense of restricted reality. Most modern societies thrive by the cultivation of illusion. In the end, such cultures of illusion may succeed in robbing the masses of their perceptual abilities to separate illusion from truth. As journalist Chris Hedges notes – 'not since the Soviet and fascist dictatorships, and perhaps the brutal authoritarian control of the Catholic Church in the Middle Ages, has the content of information been as skillfully and ruthlessly controlled and manipulated.'[1] Our so-called developed societies manufacture and peddle their illusion of reality as much as they can. And any denouncement or doubt upon this illusion is immediately met by a systemic defense that labels the critics as conspiracy theorists, anarchists, or anti-social. In other words, those who question the cultural narrative (a.k.a. illusion) are branded as deluded. This is the ultimate in perception management. And what if we all *did* go crazy – what then? Reality, it seems, is that which the majority believe, as shown here in a revised version of an ancient tale:

> *There was once a powerful President who ruled over his Republic in a far-off part of the globe. In these parts of the world the President acted much like a king, feeling that he was the sole authoritative ruler over his people. Democracy was certainly not high on his agenda as this President felt it more effective to rule through power than through elected vote. And so, the President was feared, and none dare speak out against him for there were no free speech in a country where the media worked for the President.*
>
> *Now it happened that whilst the President ruled powerfully over the land he failed to recognize that his weakness lay right beneath his very feet.*
>
> *One night an old man, who was a known and respected chemist in the capital city, snuck into the main water plant that supplied the city and its environs. While those in the city were sleeping, and without any of the guards of the water plant suspecting, he poured a strange brew into the main water system. The old chemist sighed, for he was tired of his President and the crazy authority he had placed over his once proud land.*

'From now on, anyone who drinks this water really will go crazy,' he said. And he left, knowing that the next day he too would drink of the same water.

The next morning all the inhabitants opened their taps and began drinking the water supplied from the main water plant – except the President who always drank from bottled water. Over the coming days everyone went crazy, as the chemist had predicted. Soon enough all the people had become crazy and began going through the streets and gathering in public places protesting against the President. Openly, and without fear, they called out:

'The President is mad. He has lost his reason and is no longer fit to rule us. We must oust him – down with the President! Soon people were gathering outside of his palace with large placards reading 'The President is crazy – The People are sane.'

The President ordered an investigation, but everyone thought he was crazy. Without the passive compliance of the people the President realized he had no real power – and this made him feel really mad. In his anger he became thirsty and, in his haste, and without his servants to supply his bottled water, he opened his own taps and drank from them.

The next day everything became clear. He realized that it was he, after all, who had the situation all wrong. Everything, of course, was a matter of perspective – he knew that now.

Soon after that there was great rejoicing across the Republic because the President had regained his sanity, and everything was back in balance again – and everyone was content...or so they all reasoned.

It has been said that when a culture, and its people, become unmoored from reality then they retreat into a world of fantasy. And then this fantasy mode can invert meanings, truths, and all sense of what is going on. Such collective illusions - or 'bubble realities'- can feed the populace on trigger words and phrases like *war on terror* or *yes, we can* or *make us great again*, and within these narrow hypnotic parameters all critical thought, ambiguity, and conscious observation vanish. And when the people can no longer distinguish between what is truth and what is fiction (make believe), then reality gets usurped and the fantasy world takes over.

An epidemic of information can just as easily turn into a pandemic of misinformation. In many ways it already has. Information has always been used as a tool of psychological warfare as it forms a part of state-sponsored operations that serve as a new back door into peoples' minds. Once false information is planted inside of our minds then it becomes harder to be objective or to make clear distinctions. Such information can then easily be hash-tagged, trended, and go viral. Going viral is now a common word, used to denote things, both positive and negative, that have gained rapid, and often unexpected, popularity. The word viral used to signify the behavior of a virus; that is, a small, infectious agent. The analogy is an apt one – agents of infection are now constantly roaming our information networks and entering into our minds. Information we receive is likely to be infected with a 'viral agent' just like coughing can and does spread the common cold. And one of the largest spreaders of 'thought viruses' today is social media. The social media, with customized targeting of news and adverts, is increasingly reinforcing the opinions, viewpoints, and beliefs we have already chosen to accept rather than presenting us with challenging new ones. We end up reinforcing our own bubbles of perception instead of expanding them.

The criteria and legitimacy of truth has been substituted by the promotion of incredulous untruths throughout our media systems. We now have a serious credibility issue with our major social institutions – media, politics, education, and finance. The mainstream media now represents the triumphant illusionism; the ambiguity of the spectacle that deceives and anaesthetizes the imagination. The gradual, uniform bombardment of information has succeeded in leveling out difference and now much of the content comes across as being almost the same. Diversity is just a superficial sleight-of-hand distraction. It doesn't really matter which mainstream news channel a person tunes into; they are all getting their information from a very limited selection of sources. Information is dispersed from a very tightly centralized sphere of power.

Media Centralization

These days most western media organizations are owned by only a handful of giant conglomerates. These giant corporations include Comcast; Disney; Time Warner; News Corp; Viacom; Vivendi Universal; and Bertelsmann. Over the years they have continued to absorb rival companies – called mergers – that expand their broadcasting reach. Comcast is currently the world's largest broadcasting company, with MSNBC, CNBC, Universal Pictures, and is the largest home Internet service provider in the United States. Disney (The Walt Disney Company) is the second largest entertainment and media multinational in the world. Disney owns the TV networks ABC, Disney Channel, ESPN, A&E, and the History Channel, as well as publishing, merchandising, and theatre subsidiaries. They also own Walt Disney Pictures, Touchstone Pictures, Hollywood Pictures, Miramax Film

Corp., Dimension, and Buena Vista International, as well as 11 theme parks around the world. Oh yes, and they recently bought the famous Star Wars franchise too. Currently the world's third largest mass media entertainment conglomerate, after Comcast and Disney, is Time Warner, Inc. Time Warner owns more than 50 magazines; a film studio as well as various film distributors; more than 40 music labels (including Warner Bros, Atlantic, and Elektra); and several TV networks (such as HBO, Cartoon Network, and CNN).

Similarly, Viacom owns TV networks CBS, MTV, VH1, Nickelodeon, Comedy Central, Paramount Pictures, and nearly 2000 cinema screens, as part of their media empire. And Vivendi Universal owns 27% of US music sales via labels such as Interscope, Geffen, A&M, Island, Def Jam, MCA, Mercury, Motown and Universal. They also own Universal Studios, Studio Canal, Polygram Films, Canal+, and numerous Internet and mobile phone companies. Then there is Bertelsmann which, as a global media corporation, runs Europe's second largest TV, radio and production company (the RTL Group) with 45 TV stations and 32 radio channels; Europe's largest printing and publishing firm (Gruner & Jahr); the world's largest

English-language general trade book publisher (Random House); the world's largest book and music club group (Direct Group); and an international media and communications service provider (Arvato AG).

I'm fairly sure the average person will not have heard of Charter Communications. Are they famous? Are they big? They are the second-largest cable operator in the United States, just behind Comcast, and the third largest pay-TV operator. In 2015 Charter bought out Time-Warner Cable in a deal valued at 78.7 billion dollars. Now that's big. Yet perhaps more well-known in the public eye is News Corp which combines a vast range of TV and satellite channels, magazine and newspaper holdings, record companies and publishing companies based worldwide, with a strong presence in Asian markets. Are we getting the picture? The world of entertainment is controlled by huge megalithic conglomerates who absorb (sorry, merge) with rival competition.

After the corporations, perhaps the next biggest source of news these days is the aptly anonymous 'government source' that peddles the same swindle of news to all consumers. Whatever happened to the trusted source? The public would like to know – who killed Kennedy, and who killed 'the source'? These days all we have are the surrogates, the flat substitutes. We have Associated Press and Reuters News that have swallowed up the plethora of sources that once validated the flow of information. News is now spat-out in friendly sound-bites so not as to bore the impatient consumer. News has become increasingly those 'vanishing events' that are transient occurrences and then leave without lasting traces in our memory. Who was that person who got stabbed while shopping the other day? Who left their dog in the car on a hot day until a passer-by smashed the window? Who was it in the news who got falsely arrested, falsely accused, and then quietly released? Who was that cop who got shot? Who won the last series of X-Factor or You've-Got-Talent, etc, etc? Or was it the cop who shot someone else whom the authorities don't care about? Ah yes, it was the 'transient-news-person' that has slipped back into the no-sphere.

In the US especially, television journalism has become a masquerade. Chris Hedges notes that 'Television journalism is largely a farce. Celebrity reporters, masquerading as journalists, make millions a year and give a platform to the powerful and the famous so they can spin, equivocate, and lie...If you are a true journalist, you should start to worry if you make $5 million a year.’[2] In this manner, personalized tidbits, intimate stories of stars, politicians, and the celebrity elite are passed off as news in order to distract us. Such crass journalism seeks out not stories of depth or worth but a fantasy roundabout of personalities. And the more ‘larger-than-life’ the stories then the more chance they have of success and of being taken into people’s hearts. Stories that reflect these ‘celebrity’ personalities get media attention, especially when saturated in gossip, relationships, or domestic struggles. Personalities are less adored when they go marching against fracking practices or oil pipeline proposals. Somehow it just doesn’t feel right that a beautiful star from a movie franchise should be protesting in a jumpsuit and sneakers in the rain. The two images just don’t go together well in people’s heads.

Information itself has now become its own form of stagecraft. And most of the news in today’s modern world is booby-trapped.

Newsflash: news is fake

Today’s information and news is more about perception

management than it is about educating the people. Influencing minds is more favorable, and more lucrative, than informing them. The end result is both more guaranteed and more controlled. Open information has always been a dangerous thing, as religious and social institutions have long known. Controlled information seeks to create contrived headlines, censored and cut images, and sanitized news. And as consumers of such news we are accepting and buying into an encroaching unrealism. It is a world of substitution that subverts the mind. It is often easier to confuse and misinform than it is to inculcate opinion.

Today we are faced with a new type of news. We have entered a mirror hall of journalism where fake news and alternative facts are further obscuring the veneer of truth by tampering with the already fragile and fragmented sense of reality. The malady of the unreal is spreading like a pandemic. Fake is the new 'new'!

In the last couple of years, the meme of 'alternative facts' has been gaining ground, especially in political talk. It is a convenient way of brushing off inconvenient news as well as appearing to discredit the source of the information. Not only that, it is also a deliberate way to add confusion to the issue. Once people begin to question the validity of reported news and the 'facts of the truth' then no one can be sure again of what is real or not. This appeared to be a political tactic during the 2016 US presidential campaign, especially on the part of the Republican nominee Donald Trump (who subsequently became president). Not only did Trump like to refer to inconvenient news as 'alternative facts' but he also cultivated a habit (whether consciously or not) of contradicting himself and being inconsistent in his policies. In the end it proved confusing for journalists to pin him down, and social media was rife with a flood of contradictory statements, opinions, and criticism. Nobody really knew what Trump stood for either politically or personally; and in the end not only did it not seem to matter to many, but the uncertainty and confusion most likely worked in his favor.

In a similar manner it was noted by astute commentators that the Putin government in Russia also plays the 'uncertainty card' by playing all sides of the political game. In his documentary *Hypernormalization* Adam Curtis points out that the Putin regime backed and supported many of their political opponents and critical factions, unbeknown to the factions themselves, and then exposed this tactic publicly. The result was that credibility in the political domain was eroded and in its wake was left uncertainty and confusion. The role of 'truth' was no longer viable. It is hard for anyone to discern what is real and what is credible information when the playing field is deliberately manipulated with misinformation. A similar strategy has been used by governmental spy agencies the world over. In fact, it would be fair to say that a great deal of mainstream information currently in circulation is misinformation. That is, it has been tampered, doctored, censored, or falsified. Perhaps the only real 'truth' is that which comes through personal experience. The rest is a fabrication of the world. The recent much-publicized phenomenon of 'fake news' is not something new, only that once upon a time it was under controlled dispersion and called mainstream news.

Social media, especially since the 2016 US presidential elections, has been dealing with the rise of fake news. People have been setting up online news sites, copying information from other sites, adapting the news angle according to political bias, and then posting them out with fancy open-source videos and clickbait headlines. Ah yes, that's another phenomenon which has just sprung up – clickbaits. These are catchy headlines that get people clicking on them, usually under false pretenses, only in order to generate ad revenue. As one such clickbait news author confessed in an interview – 'The ability to write a clickbaity headline, toss in some user-generated video found on YouTube, and dash off a 400-word post in 15 to 30 minutes is a skill they don't teach in journalism school.'[3] Many fake news sites were popping up during the election months in peripheral locations outside of the target country. One such notable example during the US Presidential election campaign was the flood of fake news websites that appeared in a small city in Macedonia where sensationalist news created huge advertising revenues. One of those responsible, a nineteen-year-old Macedonian student, commented that – 'The Americans loved our stories and we make money from them...Who cares if they are true or false?'[4]

Who cares, indeed? Education used to be about acquiring knowledge. In a world of post-truth and 'alternative facts' there is no validity to knowledge. Nowadays that which is classed as knowledge is more often data-information that has been agreed upon for general dissemination. Even the phenomenon of so-called 'leaks' is just another faked pseudo-news event. We often hear that some pressing news has been 'leaked' from government sources, or some such authority, as if this was not meant to happen. Yet most of us know that this is just a modern public relations strategy to either test a story out on the public to gauge reaction, or to prepare the public for some future preordained event. Leaking is rarely ever the true leaking variety – it is just another way of releasing controlled or tampered information. One example (one from many) is when the US government, prior to the first invasion of Iraq, leaked 'top-secret intelligence' to the press so that the following day they could speak about it on national television because it was already in the public domain. This occurred in the lead up to the invasion of Iraq in the US, when Dick Cheney's office 'leaked' information to the *New York Times* so they could talk about it the next day on the Sunday talk shows.[5] Such underhand tactics are used by governing institutions the world over. And this applies not only with the big global issues but also with regular everyday politics.

We find in our daily news that extracts from an upcoming political speech has been 'leaked' to the press. Why is it that the press seems to know what's upcoming in almost all of the political speeches? It's obvious to any half-serious observer that political offices pass on parts of their upcoming speeches deliberately to test the waters with their content and to prepare the public of what is to come. Leaky channels are just another name for information channels these days.

These all-too-often instances of 'legitimate' news dissemination are nothing when compared to the state-sponsored infiltrations from government agencies. The so-called 'Russiagate' scandal is just another mix of hypocrisy and misinformation. It shows a shameless level of hypocrisy in that it is well-known, and documented, that countries such as the US and China have a horde of cyber-technicians infiltrating online forums, chat sites, web gatherings, blogs, etc, and deliberately seeding and spreading a range of calculated (mis)information. This information may be pro-government propaganda, deliberate misinformation, alternative 'facts,' or downright post-truth irregularities aimed at confusing the infosphere. The information highways are an open playing field where many actors, agencies, and agendas are vying for presence, infiltration, and dominance. The game is now on in the digital realms – and it's all about the management of perception. It's hard to judge just exactly who is saying what, or why.

***Who* is saying what?**

It is going to be increasingly likely that the news you read online or from your favorite newspaper will not have been written by whom you thought it was. Take a look at this example:

> Thomas Keehn didn't allow a single run as Stags defeated Good Counsel 1-0 on Wednesday. Keehn allowed just two hits and induced a fly out from Walker to end the game.
> The pitching was strong on both sides. Thomas Keehn struck out nine, while Orie sat down three.
> Stags captured the lead in the second inning.
> A single by Grass in the second inning was a positive for Good Counsel.
> Keehn earned the win for Stags. He went seven innings, giving up zero runs, two hits, and striking out nine. Orie took the loss for Good Counsel. He tossed six innings, giving up one run, three hits, and striking out three.
> Timmy Pyne went 2-for-2 at the plate to lead Stags in hits.[3]

Maybe not the most prosaic of pieces; and it certainly will not win any literary prizes. Yet I doubt that the author will care, for it is neither a he nor a she – it is an algorithm. It was written by a powerful artificial intelligence engine, named 'Quill,' that was created by Narrative Science, Inc; a company set up to produce automated articles in a variety of areas, including sports, business, and politics.

---

[3] Taken from a randomly selected online sports website; in this case http://www.demathacatholicbaseball.com/in-the-news (accessed 25 May 2017)

This intelligence software can generate a news story approximately every thirty seconds. Many of their automated articles are already published and used by widely known and respected websites that prefer not to disclose this fact. A quick way to find articles produced by 'Quill' is to do a search using the following words - 'Powered by Narrative Science and GameChanger Media' – as I just did to find the above extract. The idea that people write all the news stories is just another illusion. At a 2011 industry conference the co-founder of Narrative Science, Kristian Hammond, predicted that the number of news articles that would be written by algorithms within fifteen years would be over ninety percent.[6]

On their homepage website Narrative Science boldly claim that:

> Narrative Science is humanizing data like never before, with technology that interprets your data, then transforms it into Intelligent Narratives at unprecedented speed and scale. With Narrative Science, your data becomes actionable—a powerful asset you can use to make better decisions, improve interactions with customers and empower your employees.[4]

---

[4] For more information see - https://www.narrativescience.com/

So, our data information is being humanized 'like never before' by taking out the human element – how's that? Well, it's just another illusion – a great sleight-of-hand and the deft art of perception management. Yet whilst it's hard to totally agree with the above prediction that in the near future over ninety percent of our news will be written by algorithms, it does show how those in the industry perceive our ever-decreasing human future. My own sense is that with the continued rise of social media there will be a healthy civil journalism from the people on the ground. There is also likely to be an increase in alternative news gathering and dissemination. Yet it does beg the question of whether we will be able to discern the difference between human-generated news and an algorithm. How would you know that something you read online was written by an algorithm or not? And this takes us to the issue of trust, which is likely to be a growing area of concern in the years ahead. As the illusion of our information intensifies the notion of trusted networks and trusted sources will become paramount. And trust is a matter of discernment.

During these bardo times we will need to strengthen our senses of discernment. Just like the original bardo where the 'in-between' worlds can be confusing, full of lost and wandering souls, so too can the social bardo down here on earth be a perplexing zone. In the Buddhist bardo realm we are told that the reincarnating soul must find its way back to the earthly realm. In the bardo times of social life we must find our way through the uncertainties, deliberate confusions, misinformation, and manipulated events. The soul, it seems, has no respite whether it is between worlds or in this world.

To have discernment means that we have an active critical faculty – and that means being alert. Alert to the sources of our news, opinions, and cultural reporting. And especially alert to what is being told (or fed) to us through our leaky political channels. We need to be alert and observe how the information is being played out through our mainstream institutional channels. Most of the news and information that will be on 'public display' through the bardo years will be directed at an emotional level. And much of this too will be a pendulum swing between trite entertainment and emotional fear (see Chapter 9). The saturated world of information in which we now live can be a rich source for us or it can be a distracting circus. It is our responsibility to decide which one we wish to make it.

In the bewildering realm of the social bardo we

are also bombarded with distractions that cater to the spoiling of the self. We are plied with commercial self-help mantras and cute cat videos (see Chapter 8). So-called 'self-development' still gets packaged into Ashram Avenue, Guru Boulevard, or sweat-room yoga. And yet we do not need these false appliances to really work on our sense of being grounded, alert, and critically aware. We need to really see what's going on, and to see through the show. We have to take out the trash before it has a chance to enter into our minds. Working on being the grounded observer is subtler than we may ever suspect. And in our increasingly carnivalesque cultures it is ever more needed, and a counter-balance to the effervescent spectacles that beguile us. The spectacle is about to get a lot more gregarious.

A Bardo Chat with: Mercury, Roman God of communication and deceit.

Author (A): Hello? Mercury, is that you?

Mercury (M): Sure is - you caught me just as I was passing through! (chuckles)

A: Great, glad to have caught you, I was…

M: Not caught! Certainly not caught – I meant I just happened to have been present, so you're lucky. You wouldn't have caught me if you'd tried, mind you.

A: Indeed. Yes, thank you. I'd just like a quick chat, if I may?

M: Sure, quick chat – go ahead.

A: Thanks. I wanted to ask you if you had anything to say about the nature of illusion; especially as it relates to us here.

M: (laughs) Ah, now that's a topic or two! Illusion, yes, what a great topic. Is it here, or is it not? Is it real, or not? Aha, illusion has been one of your principal features for you people. You think the sky is blue and the grass is green. You swear by it. Now that's an illusion!

A: Aren't they?

M: They're not from where I'm standing, but you people always insisted on your way of seeing, and everyone else's way is just plain wrong. You see according to how your brain interprets things. Since you all have the same brainy things in your heads you all more or less see the same things. Sometimes a bump on the head is not a bad thing!

(laughs)

A: So, everything is a matter of perception?

M: Sure it is. And you folks are all so gullible too. It's just so easy to fool you; as you say, to pull the wool over your eyes. You're easier to fool than the woolly mammoths, if you get my drift?

A: Certainly. And why do you think that is?

M: Well, it seems that however built you (chuckles) put in an in-built capacity for you to believe what you're told. I guess it made it easier to control you rowdy lot! But it's so true – you seem to believe whatever you hear or see. And especially if it comes from someone dressed as authority – you're all suckers for authority. All I have to do is come among you dressed in a uniform and you all get hypnotized. You don't use the inner faculty enough.

A: The inner faculty?

M: Yes - it's the faculty of true discernment that lies within you. Y'know, that voice of conscience and truth. That's also an in-built capacity but it hardly ever gets used. It's probably lying dormant, curled up in sleep! No wonder things are as they are with you all. You've stopped listening to yourselves. Now you just walk around listening to others. Well, listening to others if you're in a good mood. Most of the time you're not even listening at all! (laughs). I shake my head, I really do. That's what I'm doing now.

A: Doing what?

M: Shaking my head. Like this.

A: Oh, I can't see anything.

M: No worries - one shake is as good as another.

A: Mm, right (pause). Anyhow, do you think there are those who are deliberately trying to fool us?

M: Ah, for sure - open your eyes! Or better still, open your inner voice and listen. There are so many things going on and yet you all seem to be in a daze.

A: You mean like in a trance?

M: Whoa, yeah, that's it! You're all tranced up. I really don't know where to begin trying to get messages through to you all. I mean, real messages, not all the fakery that's going on. I do deliver real messages you know (laughs).

A: Really - it's been that hard?

M: Sure, it has. It's no wonder why all us gods left you - you stopped listening to us! Instead you all turned back to yourselves and went dumb and numb inside. You started to develop these systems of belief that told you that everything in the universe revolved around you. You started to believe that you were the masters!

A: Yes, maybe. We often refer to ourselves as 'masters of our own fate.'

M: There you go! But it's all just nonsense. You don't even know what this thing called 'fate' actually is. Yet you use the word and pass it around as if it were a common article, like bread.

A: So, what is fate then?

M: (sighs) Here we go again. Your minds are easily diverted by curiosity. You like to collect bits of information to store it away and you call it knowledge. Your species is like a keeper of miscellaneous objects. You are keepers of your own curiosity shop with thousands of things on display - hah!

A: Yes, that sounds about right. So, no clarity on fate then?

M: Not likely. It's of no use to you right now. Whatever I told you would just be stored away. You would not be able to use it. To return to the issue at hand - you are not masters of your fate. You are more like a medium for the life flow.

A: Life flow?

M: Yes. Life flows. It is an energy and a language. And it flows through you and into your world, your reality. Open yourself up to something that is more than you - that is beyond you - just for once! (laughs).

A: Okay. And how do we start doing this?

M: Really, you have to start listening. Maybe then some of us will slowly begin to come back. Meanwhile, we have other folks out there who need us. Speaking of that, I have a message I need to deliver. Got to go...best of luck with it all - and get listening to yourselves...

A: Okay, thanks Mercury - good advice! Speedy travels. Bye.

Endnotes

[1] Hedges, Chris. 2010. *Empire of Illusion: The End of Literacy and the Triumph of Spectacle*. New York: Nation Books, p45

[2] Hedges, Chris. 2010. *Empire of Illusion: The End of Literacy and the Triumph of Spectacle*. New York: Nation Books, p169

[3] 'How Facebook powers money machines for obscure political 'news' sites', *The Guardian*, https://www.theguardian.com/technology/2016/aug/24/facebook-clickbait-political-news-sites-us-election-trump, 24 August 2016 (accessed 25 May 2017)

[4] 'The city getting rich from fake news,' BBC News, http://www.bbc.com/news/magazine-38168281, 5 December 2016 (accessed 25 May 2017)

[5] Hedges, Chris. 2010. *Empire of Illusion: The End of Literacy and the Triumph of Spectacle*. New York: Nation Books, p171-3

[6] Ford, Martin. 2015. *The Rise of the Robots: Technology and the Threat of Mass Unemployment*. London: Oneworld Publications, p87.

7.

phantom performances

- the rise of the spectacle

7. phantom performances – the rise of the spectacle

ˈspɛktək(ə)l/

noun

a visually striking performance or display
an event or scene regarded in terms of its visual

Now the death of God combined with the perfection of the image has brought us to a whole new state of expectation. We are the image.

John Ralston Saul, *Voltaire's Bastards*

Magical thinking is the currency not only of celebrity culture, but also of totalitarian culture.

Chris Hedges, *Empire of Illusion*

Welcome to the spectacle. Or perhaps I should say the kind of spectacle that has become the face of entertainment that pervades our westernized cultures. The way that the spectacle succeeds is that it isn't so much about fooling us into believing its lies as real, but rather that it is *we* who ask to be fooled. We seek to suspend our sense of reality, to pursue a space of escape. The spectacle pulls us in because we lend our willingness to its agenda. If we are honest, in this post-truth age, we will admit to living in an age of spectacle. And it is from this that many of us receive our interpretation of reality. Since the middle of the 20th century onwards the 'western spectacle' has been in the form of media advertisement and propaganda. We may think that we've only recently arrived at the age of the spectacle, where Disneylandification is becoming the norm, and Super Bowls are interspersed with scantily-clad singers, and TV programs appear in the slots between advertisers. Yet the whole spectacle show has been a form of function creep ever since telecommunications first emerged as a social phenomenon. The image has been with humanity since the first dawn of our arising; from cave paintings to hieroglyphics to cuneiform clay tablets. The major difference is that today the spectacle of the image has not only gone global, but it has also gotten inside of our heads.

Western cultures especially (and the US specifically) have now made the image, the spectacle, and hence the illusion so grand, so vivid, and so persuasively realistic that they are becoming our basis of reality. We swing from one illusion to the alternative, which is still yet another grand spectacle; just as we swing from the political left to the right, believing each side is distinctly different. Yet each is a part of the same bubble that customizes our lives - they form a part of our news, our heroes, our tragedies, and our dreams. We now serve a mosaic of ideals carefully crafted as a patchwork of phantom performances. Nothing is ever real anymore except the painful extremes that pervade our daily existence: the violence, the suffering, the deprivation, the inequality, the disease. Only these fragments that create great pain become the real, and from these many of us seek refuge in a plenitude of diversions, distractions, and triviality.

Western civilization has chosen to be played out upon a grand stage where the performance – of invented storylines and scripts – runs the show. Let us take the scripted performance of globalization – wasn't this meant to be a fine example of bringing freedom, liberty, and democracy around the world? We were sold on the shiny advertisement – yet it said nothing about the colonization of power, control, and finances. Neither did it discuss the interventions into lesser powerful nations and territories, and the destabilizations from within; nor the homogeneity of culture and cultural artefacts; of ideas, ideologies, and perspectives. These are all the phantom performances that have dressed up the more brutish realities that survive underneath, nonglossed, and unrepresented by the major global agencies of power. We move through social realities that are an entanglement of signs, virtual connections, social media status, and distanced negotiations. Proximity is no longer about nearness but about who has access – and how quickly. This is all a part of the bardo times in which we find ourselves, where more and more is becoming blurred around us.

We are encouraged to project back into the world our entertainment-mediatized fantasies. People begin to act out their imaginary landscapes, often in violent and distorted ways, as young students massacre their classmates before going to eat at McDonalds. This is the hyperreal that distorts a stable reality, making it harder to gain a grounded perspective on things. People are increasingly being guided by the false totems of media-militarized-entertainment.

The media spectacle gives us our modern guiding images. This is similar to how in the Middle Ages images depicted in stained glass windows and paintings of religious torment or salvation acted to control and influence the social behavior of our ancestors. For many of us the white-bearded god above is dead, so we have media depictions of heroes, adventurers, McGyvers, celebrity-cosmetic makeovers, beauty pageants, talk shows and reality television to be our social guides. An illusory sensate reality has been erected that runs on pseudo-lives and phantom performances. Such phantom performances mask our personal failures and conveniently hide them behind a curtain of the unreal. People prefer to watch the rich and famous on television rather than face the reality of broken family lives, domestic unhappiness, personal depression, and social anxiety. Computer generated images – including the famous 'green screen' backing wall where images are invented and projected – has given us all a new substitute. Why have ice when you can have bubblegum-flavored ice-cream? Today's new mantra is that we are entitled to everything; or at least almost everything is available to be bought.

Luckily for those of us who live in the west we inhabit a world of easy-correction where we can make ourselves better if we buy certain products, ingest certain foods, and hang-out in the right yoga gyms. For every situation there is seemingly a commercial solution. We have not been abandoned, after all. In the realm of hyperreality, our fantasies are no longer an impediment to success. On the contrary, our fantasies are the portals through which we enter. All we need is for the world of the media to give us our dream. Everybody has talent, as the reality shows tell us - 'Britain's Got Talent,' 'America's Got Talent:' in fact, we've all got talent! We are all of us hidden unique performers, and the world 'out there' is begging for our arrival. This is not to be confused with the manipulation by greedy commercial enterprises that are ready to discard you as soon as your 'talent' no longer sells.

Yet the truth of the matter is that the spectacle of celebrity culture seeks commodities, not real individuals or souls. It doesn't want that we seek for any form of transcendence, illumination, or real growth. It is a world that seeks only those that feed the phantom and encourage others to do the same. It is the 'real' that gets pushed into a black hole - to become a figment of the imagination, whilst imaginary dreams take its place. Celebrity culture thrives from the very lack of inner reflection. There is no 'going within' unless it is a form of medication going down our throats. If we are brutally honest, the celebrity spectacle is an ugly specter that can be as cruel as it is superficial.

The Spectacle of Celebrity Culture

No one achieves celebrity status on their own. It is a stage performance that requires a hoard of cultural enablers; from media, marketers, promoters, agents, handlers, and a host of hungry and gullible people. It is a veritable stage of actors, with each person in it to gain something for themselves. They either seek attention, satisfaction, fame, wealth, or a combination of these. Celebrity culture has come to dominate how many of us define our sense of belonging. It has come to define how we relate to the world around us, and in this respect has disfigured our notions of social belonging and community. Celebrity culture funds and feeds our own movies inside our heads as we invent our roles and behavior. It is a culture in which very few participants are even real for a day.

We idolize celebrities and often project them as idealized forms of ourselves. And yet through this substitution we move further away from any real self-actualization. The transcendent, the real, does not do substitutes. By throwing our fantasies onto others we are diminishing our own power. In the words of one serious journalist,

> We are chained to the flickering shadows of celebrity culture, the spectacle of the arena and the airwaves, the lies of advertising, the endless personal dramas, many of them completely fictional, that have become the staple of news, celebrity gossip, New Age mysticism, and pop psychology ...in contemporary culture the fabricated, the inauthentic, and the theatrical have displaced the natural, the genuine, and the spontaneous, until reality itself has been converted into stagecraft.[1]

We are subtly pushed through the well-structured stagecraft whilst all the time thinking that it is real. Our contemporary 'death of the gods' has been replaced by a divine adoration of celebrities and celebrity culture. Celebrity items, like holy relics, are paraded, idolized, and sold for vast sums. People rush for autographs, only to sell them later on eBay to make an unhealthy profit. Celebrity personal possessions are sold off at prestigious auction houses for astronomical prices, so aging people can wear the clothes of their idols. The glitzy suit that Elvis wore before dying in a Las Vegas toilet; or the dress that Marilyn Monroe wore to show her knickers to the world above a subway vent. Everything is up for grabs - the profane is made sacred, and then sacrificed as celebrity talismans. It all engenders a performance of hysteria, leading sometimes to stalking, or what is nowadays referred to as 'trolling,' as celebrity private photos are hacked and shared online. It's happened to Emma Watson, Jennifer Lawrence, Kate Upton, Jessica Alba, Kate Hudson, Scarlett Johansson...and the list goes on, and on, and on.

The world of celebrity culture thrusts us into a moral void. People are valued by their appearance and their skin-deep beauty rather than their humanity. Such a culture focuses upon onanistic desires and ways for self-gratification. The cult of self 'has within it the classic traits of psychopaths: superficial charm, grandiosity, and self-importance; a need for constant stimulation, a penchant for lying, deception, and manipulation, and the inability to feel remorse or guilt.'[2] The cult of self also promotes the right to get whatever we wish, and celebrity media plays into this, often at the cost of the celebrity who suffers from social media harassment and online trolling. Celebrity public life is not a sacred space; instead, it has become a theatre of performance that is open for all spectators. And those spectators who surround themselves with celebrity culture tend to live in the present, fed by an endless stream of packaged information. They live by credit promises, ignorant to the future prospect of unmanageable debt. They are hostage to a culture that keeps them enthralled, like a television commercial replete with pleasing jingles. They navigate their purchases through well-known brands, eyeing the famous logos as guides. It is an image-saturated reality, bright and tantalizing, offering comfort and satisfaction upon all levels - until the credit runs out. Then the person becomes an outlaw to the very system that fattened them up like foie gras ducks.

These are the trivial diversions that for many are necessary, and which exist in cultures that prize shallow entertainment above substance. We may wonder whether the consumerist celebrity culture is a compensation for the loss of our true freedom regarding the human spirit and our well-being. And celebrities too are often trapped within their own fairy-tale prisons. They are skillfully controlled by their handlers and pushed in front of the media – all this to compensate for the insatiable appetites of those thirsty spectators that swarm upon celebrity culture. We are tantalizingly shown that even us, the humble spectators, can triumph in fame through the lens of reality television. The celebrity machinery oils itself on the media-creation of third and fourth-rate celebrities that have their fifteen minutes of fame – crammed together on desert islands, stuffing insects into their mouths as they bad-mouth their once beloved 'best-friend' and vote them off the show. Reality survival, it seems, comes at a cost. And then when they finally emerge into the 'real world' of the hyperreal they throng and mingle with other reality-stars under the glare of media spotlight in the vain hope that together they can populate an illusory world of the celebrity.

The world of reality television is another limb on the body of phantom performance. In the last decade a multitude of reality shows have cropped up on our television screens; and they all have one thing in common – they involve being constantly watched. Popular shows such as *Big Brother* put strangers to live together with round-the-clock constant surveillance. These strangers are even videoed in their beds as they sleep or fondle and kiss with other contestants. Sex lives are ogled over alongside the tears and on-screen breakdowns. Then the television psychologists are wheeled out to offer 'expert commentary' on the contestant's state for mass consumption. Yet underneath all this glamour and glitz is the subtle message that intrusive surveillance is a normal feature of contemporary societies. In fact, it even masquerades as something cool that can be shared online, and which can make us famous. However, the brute reality is that such reality shows normalize what would otherwise be blatant non-constitutional intervention. And yet such shows make surveillance not only routine but a potentially enjoyable part of our modern lives. We are being conditioned into monitoring and sharing our own lives for others to see. Our phantom performances can make any one of us into an enviable star.

Social media is now rife with home-grown videos where everyone from toddler to teenager to retiree is making their performances visible to the image-hungry collective. Selfies too are the new fashionable rage as we perform in front of ourselves. This trend has become so pervasive that each year the number of selfie-related deaths has been increasing. In 2015 more people died from taking selfies than from shark attacks.[1] A dedicated online Wikipedia page has been established to record some of the ongoing 'selfie-deaths.' Here are a few examples:

> Two young men died in the Ural Mountains after they pulled the pin from a live hand grenade to take a selfie. The phone with the picture remained as evidence of the circumstance of their deaths. (Russia, January 2015)

---

[1] See http://www.telegraph.co.uk/technology/11881900/More-people-have-died-by-taking-selfies-this-year-than-by-shark-attacks.html

A 22-year-old man was trying to recreate a scene from his favorite movie Barking at the Stars by running in front of a train, beating it and being hailed a hero. As he ran in front of the train, he tried to take a selfie to document the scene. He was killed instantly when the express train hit him at full speed in the village of Lacarak near the northern Serbian town of Sremska Mitrovica. (Serbia, April 2015)

An 18-year-old died when she attempted to take the "ultimate selfie", posing with a friend on top of a train in the north-eastern Romanian city of Iași when her leg touched a live wire above which electrocuted her with 27,000 volts. (Romania, May 2015)

A man was gored to death in the annual bull-running festival in the town of Villaseca de la Sagra while trying to take a selfie with a bull. (Spain, August 2015)

A 19-year-old from Houston died after trying to take an Instagram selfie while holding a loaded gun to his head. He accidentally fired the gun and shot himself in the throat. (USA, September 2015)

A 17-year-old student, Andrey Retrovsky from Vologda, Russia, fell to his death attempting to take a selfie while hanging from a rope from a nine-story building. The rope snapped. Retrovsky was known for taking 'extreme' selfies and posting them to his Instagram account. (Russia, September 2015)

Five teenagers laid down in the middle of the road near an airport to take a selfie with a plane landing in the background. It was at night, and a truck driver did not see them and accidentally ran them over, killing two of them. (Turkey, December 2015)

> In southern Nepal, a truck driver stopped for a wild herd of 21 elephants crossing the road. The driver exited his vehicle to take a selfie with the animals. The herd attacked and killed the man. (Nepal, July 2016)
>
> At Alwal Railway station near Secunderabad, India, a man died while another lost his hand when the duo was run over by a moving train while clicking selfies on Tuesday (India, May 2017)[3]

Selfie deaths, it seems, are global – and not a rare occurrence. Our phantom performances come at a cost. In a world where the image is iconic, more and more people are losing themselves in a reality where a sense of achievement comes from catching the 'ultimate selfie.'

The new trend, or zeitgeist of our age, is visibility. As one educationist laments:

> The camera has created a culture of celebrity; the computer is creating a culture of connectivity. As the two technologies converge - broadband tipping the Web from text to image; social-networking sites spreading the mesh of interconnection ever wider - the two cultures betray a common impulse. Celebrity and connectivity are both ways of becoming known. This is what the contemporary self wants. It wants to be recognized, wants to be

> connected: It wants to be visible. If not to the millions, on *Survivor* or *Oprah*, then hundreds, on Twitter or Facebook. This is the quality that validates us, this is how we become real to ourselves - by being seen by others. The great contemporary terror is anonymity.[4]

The drive for inner fulfilment, transcendence, and growth has been wavered aside in favor of the spectral pixilated image. We fear not being seen. We dread being anonymous. Even being a ghost is preferable to being dead.

Spectral Forms: Image Culture & Ghosting

The new perspective on the world is pixilated. We are awash with images without substance and which are routinely fetishized as iconic. Signs are lacking immanence; they are fleeting and transient like never before. That is why corporations spend millions trying to find an image logo that will stick around long enough to be implanted into our minds. Images are becoming signs to the disappearance of the real. Images are the new believable reality; now no one cares that the original behind the image has quietly slipped away. The world exists as if in a play of phantom appearances. The image has taken centerstage within the space of the new real.

Yet the danger here is that in being given the image with its glamour and glitz we are in return giving up our critical and intellectual tools that help us cope with a complex world. Where once we had the faculty of separating illusion from reality we now have a simplified hyperreal world where everything can be explained away by a platitude of post-truth phrases. Does it even matter anymore that Las Vegas with its illusion of France with the mock Eiffel Tower, or its pseudo-canals of Venice, are far from the reality of France or Venice? How many people care? Or that the fantasy worlds within the various Disney theme parks are merging with the entertainment-saturated lives outside? Would it truly matter if we were all living within a controlled environment as depicted within the film *The Truman Show*? (see Chapter 12 for more on this). Or maybe, just maybe, such films are actually trying to tell us something - to wake us up.

The danger now is that our cultural spectacles – our celebrity culture and spectral images – are making any other alternative seem dull to us. It may be that in an age of simplified gratification any complex reality is boring. What the 'real' presents us with may no longer be enough. We are now craving for the 'beyond real' – even beyond death. Welcome to the new world of *ghosting*.

In the modern world of fast relationships and even faster communications the term 'ghosting' (adj) came to be known as the act of behaving as if nothing is wrong and then completely disappearing out of someone's life without a trace. There is no phone call, no texting, no Whatsapp or Facebook tagging – nil, nothing, zero. It's as if the person is no longer in existence and you never even knew them. This type of behavior still very much goes on, of course, but now the term 'ghosting' has a newer connotation. In the age of technical trickery and CGI (computer-generated images) the magical movie makers are now able to conjure up actors from beyond the grave.

Ghosting in this context refers to how CGI in the movie business is able to create actors on the screen after they are dead. At this stage they re-create a digital likeness of the person and place it over a stand-in actor who is acting out the other's performance in front of the legendary green screen. This is also referred to as 'digital resurrection,' and it is becoming an increasingly popular strategy in contemporary films. A recent example of this was the Star Wars film *Rogue One* (2016) which wanted to bring back the original character of Grand Moff Tarkin (first played by British actor Peter Cushing in 1977). The film makers also wanted to bring back the original actor, Cushing, in order to create a sense of continuity. However, the problem here was that Cushing had died in 1994. No problem – movies can bring to life a phantom performance.

For the film they took archive footage and a digital scan of Peter Cushing's face that had been made years earlier for a previous film, and from this they created a 3D CGI mask that was augmented and adapted for a stand-in actor.[2] In order to achieve a correct vocal imitation the movie makers searched through hours of footage from the original 1977 Star Wars film to build up material. The result was an impressive 'digital resurrection' of actor Peter Cushing (deceased) acting out a film role twenty-four years after his death. Although movies had made use of CGI tactics previously to cover up scenes where actors had suddenly died before filming had ended, none of them had been as impressive as the digital resurrection

---

2 In this case the stand-in actor was the English stage and screen actor Guy Henry.

achieved in *Rogue One*.[3] There can be no greater example of a phantom performance than the spectacle of bringing the dead back to digital life. In such a performance there is no real presence or time. The 'reality' of this person on screen has no origin of their arrival, no presence, and no connection to our known world. They are as a ghostly doppelganger stalking our screens. And now that the doppelganger is firmly out-of-the-bag we should expect further digital phantom performances in the future. These are like scenes from our hyperreality where the 'real' is no longer the principal actor.

Our cultures are being infiltrated by the dislocated fragments of digital resurrection that form the phantoms that populate our modern haunted lives. Or perhaps it is we who are becoming more and more the phantom performers? There is the danger here that we retreat into our illusions, trapped by commodity dreams. As one astute commentator dryly notes,

> Mass culture is a Peter Pan culture. It tells us that if we close our eyes, if we visualize what we want, if we have faith in ourselves, if we tell God that we believe in miracles, if we tap into our inner strength, if we

---

[3] A famous example here is director Ridley Scott's use of CGI in the film *Gladiator* (2000) to film the final scenes of English actor Oliver Reed who had died of a heart attack during production.

> grasp that we are truly exceptional, if we focus on happiness, our lives will be harmonious and complete. This cultural retreat into illusion, whether peddled by positive psychologists, Hollywood, or Christian preachers, is a form of magical thinking. [5]

Magical thinking is not always the same as inspired thinking. Magical thinking in the context here can be informed by pseudo-events of celebrity culture, media-peddled gossip, and saccharine trivia. These are the signs of a world going through a bardo period, where a congealed mass of commodity culture tries to appease us. These are the distractions meant to turn our attention away from the magician's sleight-of-hand trick. And the tricks are happening all around us, as our societies try to rearrange themselves to prepare for a post-bardo time. Yet right now we are in the thick of it. We have to stay inspired – and inspire others – as the spectacles swirl all around us.

An Inspired Performance

The arts have served to inspire us over our long history; to deliver subtle, and often hidden, messages of inner growth and revelation. The great artistic spectacles of antiquity were often emblems that sought to trigger us to transcend beyond our lowly states. Cathedrals, monuments, paintings, theatrical performances, and great literature stood as lanterns to the human potential for development. Many great works of artistic, spiritual, and mystical literature have acted to stimulate our left-right hemispheric brain activity. Many fairy tales, children's stories, as well as humorous folk tales, riddles, and fantastical, magical tales, served to stimulate not only the human imagination but also our left-right brain interlocking hemispheres. Artistic expressions of sounds (music, chanting, and singing); light (both natural light and produced light such as in stained glass); and language (specific recitations as in mantras and zikrs) aimed at activating and developing the human potential. We have been surrounded by stimulating triggers throughout human history. At the same time retrogressive social forces which seek to hinder, distort, or derail human development have also been prevalent in our cultures.

The institutions and organizational thinking that create and push the superficial spectacles upon us wish to keep the general populace absorbed and distracted within numbing commodity cultures. Yet by such distractions we are held compliant within a simulated reality of phantom performances – and this is precisely the confusion of the bardo times. It is like strolling in fog or meandering aimlessly in a dense mist whilst not knowing how close true reality may be. We have lost touch with that essential something that can work like magic in our lives. As one thinker recently stated:

> We live in changing times whereby humanity is undergoing a transformation…We need to understand phenomena at deeper levels, and not just accept what we are told, or what is fed to us through well-structured social institutions and channels. We must learn to accept that our thinking is a great tangible spiritual force for change. [7]

We can work through these bardo years by being aware of the social and cultural forces that surround us, and which try to infiltrate into every crack and domain of our lives. Each insight gained may not appear significant, yet each serves to widen the crack where some real light can get in. We need to be on the lookout like never before in this strange domain where the online world of cute cats reign.

A Bardo Chat with: Saraswati, Hindu goddess of knowledge, music, arts, wisdom and learning

Author (A): Hello Saraswati. It is indeed an honor to speak with you.

Saraswati (S): (sounds of soft music) Hello! Greetings and blessings upon you.

A: Thank you. I wonder if you may honor me with a brief chat?

S: Words and speech are what I bring to your world, amongst many other gifts that are your inheritance. Of course – speak on!

A: Thank you. I notice that you bring so many gifts, such as learning, music, and the arts. These are indeed wonders for our world. And yet sometimes I get to wondering why it is that so many of these gifts are misused or diluted into trivial forms. Does this not displease you?

S: (giggles) Perhaps you do not know your own world as well as we do. What you speak of is expected to be the case. Not every seed that is planted comes to fruition. So many seeds are planted in the knowledge that a few of them will find their roots and grow into wondrous delights.

A: So, you are aware of how some of the arts are being commoditized and trivialized in our cultures?

S: Yes, of course. This is also the nature of your world. It is a dense realm, and the finer substances that enter will become dense and crystallized with time. That is why knowledge and learning, and knowledge of the arts, are constantly updated. Nothing stays still in your realm. Music must keep flowing, following the rivers of adaptation and mutation that pass on their learning and mastery to each upward flow. Some of this flow of learning gets trapped at the side of the river; this is the silt that falls as sediment and which at times blocks and hinders the flow. Yet eventually the flow will win out, for it is carried along with a stronger force. The sediment will get absorbed into your terrestrial earth and become recycled, and again it will attempt to move along with the river towards its rightful destination.

A: So, you are saying that the flow of the arts and learning will continue throughout our world, despite the solidifications that we see.

S: This is indeed the case – it always has been and will always be. Many of your human institutions focus solely upon the heavy sediments of culture and learning, and not upon the lightness of its flow. Often your focus is upon the mortal remains, the traces that only hint at the wonders of wisdom. As a species you are beguiled and enamored by the heavy, dirty things. Seek out the lightness; seek to immerse yourselves in the flow.

A: Yes, I understand this. And yet the heavy, coarse aspects of the arts are what are thrust upon us. Many people find it hard to escape this world of the dense stuff that surrounds us all the time.

S: This is your own excuse. The world of permanent wisdom flows through you and your world ceaselessly. All you need is to give it your proper attention. There is laziness in many of you upon your world, and this makes you turn away from the wonders. All you need to do is learn how to see. Over time you have closed down your senses. Your window onto reality is so small it only allows in a slither of sunlight and spirit. Imagine yourself in your house. If you are looking through a small window you will only see a small percentage of what lies outside. You have done the same with your senses of reality. And within this short spectrum you see more of the dense, solidified forms, and less of the lightness.

A: We need to open our senses then?

S: This and much more. It is not only about being open. You need also to be aware.

A: Could you explain the difference here?

S: If you are open you see more things. Yet without awareness you are unable to understand what you see. It is like seeing a shape far in the distance. You know something is there, but you are unable to perceive it. without this perception you cannot know its function, or what you must do. You are seeing, but you are helpless. Once you begin to be open, to allow your senses to perceive, you then need to develop your awareness.

A: I understand what you are saying, in theory. But how can we develop this awareness?

S: First you need to clean yourselves out (giggles). You are so cluttered inside.

A: With things?

S: (laughs) With thoughts! Your ideas, beliefs, and everything. You surround yourselves with filters. You grow up building your filters around you. Wisdom is about knowing how to let go. Knowledge is a river and wisdom are the waters that flow through it. If the rivers become blocked, then the waters cannot flow. Your beliefs are like the rocks and branches that fall into the river and disrupt the flow of the water. They are obstacles. And your fixed ideas become the obstacles within you.

A: Yes, that makes sense.

S: Oh, wise you! (giggles). You are surrounded by many waters and you can choose within which one you wish to swim. Do not blame others for your own choices.

A: Thank you – that is uplifting news.

S: You can be uplifted and carried by the flow at all times, despite the severity of your circumstances. Never forget the capacity to choose. Wisdom is like the music of the spheres. It is ever flowing. Your cosmos is built upon music. Consider this and you shall learn much. Now – choose wisely in your steps. I leave you here. Blessings to you.

A: Blessings and goodbye.

Endnotes

[1] Hedges, Chris. 2010. *Empire of Illusion: The End of Literacy and the Triumph of Spectacle*. New York: Nation Books, p15

[2] Hedges, Chris. 2010. *Empire of Illusion: The End of Literacy and the Triumph of Spectacle*. New York: Nation Books, p33

[3] https://en.wikipedia.org/wiki/List_of_selfie-related_injuries_and_deaths - accessed June 7, 2017

[4] William Deresiewicz, 'The End of Solitude,' *The Chronicle of Higher Education* 55:21 (30th January, 2009): B6

[5] Hedges, Chris. 2010. *Empire of Illusion: The End of Literacy and the Triumph of Spectacle*. New York: Nation Books, p190

[6] Gulbekian, S.E. 2004. *In the Belly of the Beast: Holding Your Own in Mass Culture*. Charlottesville, VA: Hampton Roads, p251

8.

pop spirit

- cute cats and simulated desires

8. pop spirit - cute cats & simulated desires

ˈspɪrɪt/
noun

the non-physical part of a person which is the seat of emotions and character.

False teachers and deceived seekers vainly pursue the desert vapor - and wearied return, the dupe of their own imagination.

Shahabudin Suhrawardi

A moment of enlightenment is of no use to someone who needs a good week of it.

Idries Shah

We may need more than a week of enlightenment, yet in our modern cultures all we get are bite-sized Youtube-compatible fleeting moments. The prevailing quality and mood of our bardo times is one where the 'spirit' is like the radio-friendly three-minute pop song. It is a digestible burst that we can chew on without it giving us indigestion. We have literally thousands of online videos showing us how to improve almost every aspect of our lives by breathing, body postures, mental exercises, visualizations, and the good old self-to-mirror pep talks. We are told that we 'create our own reality,' despite the obvious fact that in many countries we have accepted sociopaths in power – or perhaps we voted them into office? If that is our reality, then what does it say about ourselves – that most of us are latent sociopaths with a hidden agenda for inflicting suffering upon others? Or that what we secretly desire is a plenitude of crass media and commercialized, corporate entertainment? If this is creating our own reality, then most of us must also be secretly longing for therapy.

It seems that the sublime has become lost or distorted within the grotesque spectacle of the spirit. That is, aspects of our soul nature have become commoditized and watered down so that they are shards or filaments of their real glory. And modern cultures worship these shards as if the fleeting reflections that fall from them are profound insights. Totems once considered sacred are splashed across social media and shared as if spreading them brings us amplified gratification. Phrases of some truth are gobbled rapidly as we scroll down the various quote-images that fill our media feeds. We breakfast on these handy spirit pop-tarts; yet we hardly have time to consume their words of wisdom. We yearn only for the quick fix, the morning shot of 'feel good' wisdom packaged with a pleasing image, be it nirvana, Samadhi, or some surreal bliss. Colorful figures in lotus positions with flowers blossoming from their chakras adorn our virtual walls and our desktops; we have their presence programmed as our screen images. Transcendence comes through the third eye as it sits in the center of the forehead awaiting patiently its activation through social-media triggers. And if the colorful chakras in the lotus position don't get you, then there are countless videos of cute cats to make you go all fluffy and tingly inside. Whilst serious videos online only receive moderate viewing figures, the ones of cat compilations or a cute cat trying to do yoga will get in excess of ten million hits. So, in response to this truly amazing 21st century online phenomenon I posted the following on my Facebook page in April 2017:

Believe me when I tell you I was not being jealous of all those cute cat videos. Yet seriously, how could I compete? As they say – if you can't beat them, join them!

Popular cultures the world over have become saccharine playgrounds where fads and aspartame-coated famous-wannabes parade and trot like peacocks. At times, western cultures that are saturated with entertainment appear autistic; or may very well seem autistic to outside observers. This inevitably gives a bad name to those people genuinely affected by autism. We are in danger of becoming submerged in the sickly successes of such pop cultures, where the spirit is exposed as a short-cut trip to enlightenment. Of course, there is also ample room for those parodies that make light fun of such pseudo-spirit pretensions. And there are many of these humorous parodies out there in the world too. Thankfully they can make us laugh at the things we take so seriously. And we are taking so many more things seriously these days. No, seriously – we really are!

Searching where the Light is

You may think that staring into a mirror, growling to yourself and saying, 'You are a lion, rarrh!' is sort of weird, in a surreal, onanistic sort of way. But we've been told to do it, or something similar, in a myriad of books on how to develop the spiritual self. We've also been urged to call out to the universe and order what we want to arrive in our lives, naming it as 'cosmic ordering.' It's all part of the new quantum reality we live in, or so we are told by 'experts' in the quantum field (which is more often people who have taught themselves Life Coaching from an online course). And yet here there is the question of what I term the 'Quantum Dilemma;' which is this – why has quantum physics, in over a century of examination, not made any practical impact on our daily relationship with reality and the cosmos? The understanding that our reality is energy-based and responsive to observation (the observer effect) should have torn down our walls of reality-construction. And yet instead what we got were new-agey fluffball books on the likes of 'quantum-ordering' and how to ask the cosmos for our own riches and fantasized lifestyles. We know there is something strange going on over there in the dark (dark energy, dark matter) but we don't truly wish to look for it as it's easier to stay in the mainstream light. There's a story on this from the incomparable Mulla Nasrudin, and it goes like this:

> Someone saw Nasrudin searching for something on the ground.
> 'What have you lost, Mulla?' he asked.
> 'My key,' said the Mulla. So they both went down on their knees and looked for it.
> After a time the other man asked: 'Where exactly did you drop it?'
> 'In my own house.'
> 'Then why are you looking here?'
> 'There is more light here than inside my own house.'[1]

Inside of our own house is often where we choose not to look. It is too dark, and the discoveries, should they come, are bound to be too close to home – quite literally! Perhaps it would help us if we adorned the house a little. Maybe a talisman here, a crystal there, or any other number of paid-for objects and trinkets that have been imported from elsewhere and now peddled in western markets and online stores. I remember my own father telling me that back in his day a well-known cure for a rotten tooth was tying a piece of thin string around it, then tying the other end of the string to a door handle and having someone quickly slam the door shut. Whoosh – out pops the tooth! Was it his idea of perpetuating an urban myth from his own childhood (he swore it was a true story)? Yet the question is, would you or I try this method today? Despite my well-known dislike of going to the dentist, I would surely prefer a civilized visit rather than slamming my cheek up against a door, followed by a surge of pain and the dribble of blood. And yet some contemporary popular spiritual (pop spirit) practices and rituals seem to me like opting for the antiquated 'tooth-door-slam' method.

What is less well-known is the concept that spiritual practices that were once legitimate can lose their functionality if they are taken out of their original context of time and place. Then, even worse, is when such precise tools are used in a haphazard way, such as combining different elements into a new and modern groovy pop-spirit assemblage. When symbols of 'higher learning' become atrophied – meaning they are no longer adapted to the culture, the time, and the people – they often incite a 'Pavlovian' dog response on the part of the practitioners. Pop spirit emblems, symbols, and trinkets are easily transferred into fetish totems. This is similar to how the Abrahamic religion of Rastafari came to be symbolized by the trendy poster of Bob Marley smoking a fat reefa that was sticky-taped onto tens of thousands of student's bedsit walls. The two things are just not the same: emotional totems do not constitute the real thing. Popular spirituality – today's pop spirit - has become its own marketplace in the modern world. An old saying comes to mind here – *The bird which knows not of sweet water has his beak in salt water all the year.*

The pop spirit marketplace is hot - it offers exorbitant choice in the belief that more is good. This encourages some people to take, experiment, taste, and dabble with a rag-bag bunch of spiritual goodies in the hope that the resulting fusion will develop their 'essential self.' Whilst there are sincere and genuine developmental tools and practices in the world, the online social media-sphere becomes the window-displays for attractive quotations, phrases, and slogans that are hungrily consumed by a fast-paced crowd. It is easier to 'like' and 'share' a spiritual tool these days than to consider its use. Pop spirit, like breakfast pop tarts, are tastily consumable, although high in sugary fats. The modern media marketplace delivers an easy 'on-demand' lifestyle which is making us lazy and complacent in that we are used to receiving what we request; and either immediately or within 24-hours. Pop spirit fits nicely onto this conveyor belt of spiritual-supply goodies. There are plentiful videos of some young, attractive person telling us how to reach inside for that 'something higher' as they have a clean beach and rolling waves in the background. The commodity spirit tells us that having one hundred thousand subscribers is a good sign of the health of the soul. Spreading the Holy Spirit these days gets rated by rising subscribers and on how many people click the thumbs up.

The contemporary world of pop spirit is mainly a material one as it is based in terms of transaction. That is, those involved usually want to get something in exchange for something else. It's a trade-off, and a commercial one at that. It is a form of seeking that has yet to learn the fundamentals. There is a story which tells of a spiritual seeker who after some time comes upon a spiritual master that she feels is genuine and whom she wishes to learn from. The seeker asks the master if he will accept her as a pupil.

'Why do you seek a spiritual path?' asks the teacher.

'Because I wish to be a generous and virtuous person; I

wish to be balanced, mindful, caring, and to be in service for humanity. This is my goal' said the seeker.
'Well', replied the teacher, 'these are not goals on the spiritual path; these are the very basics of being human which we need before we even begin to learn'.

Pop spirit may make us feel better as we scroll down the feel-good quotes over breakfast – but will it last until lunch time? Our daily fix of uplifting quotes and video blessings may not be an antidote to the missing essentials. Contemporary societies with their surface acquisitions and quick-fix remedies may only be glossing over the type of hollowness that T.S. Eliot described post-World War 1:

We are the hollow men
We are the stuffed men
Leaning together
Headpiece filled with straw. Alas!
Our dried voices, when
We whisper together
Are quiet and meaningless
As wind in dry grass
Or rats' feet over broken glass
In our dry cellar...

... This is the way the world ends
This is the way the world ends
This is the way the world ends
Not with a bang but a whimper.

Yet despite this hollow dullness, with its dried voices and meaningless whispers, we appear to have a great amount of happiness.

Happy, Happy, Joy, Joy

There is a new wave arising and it is lifting all the sad little boats that were moored at lonely harbors with chipped paintwork. This new joy comes with its own language, rolling off the tongues of its adherents - 'I can count on others,' 'I feel autonomous,' 'I learned something new today,' and 'I did what I do best.' It makes us ask ourselves piercing and profound questions too, raising our awareness. Do we 'learn to fail or fail to learn?' and why must we say, 'it happened for the best' when we can say 'how can I make the best of what happened?' Yes, it is all about being positive in a mental kind of way.

Positive Psychology is now a growing field that is an academic discipline, a corporate strategy, as well as an ideology. The video presentations are already widely dispersed online, and a range of books cater to this positive tool. Books include titles such as *Born to be Good: The Science of the Meaningful Life*; *Authentic Happiness;*

Happier: Learn the Secrets to Daily Joy and Lasting Fulfillment. Positive Psychology comes with academic credibility; the Positive Psychology Center at the University of Pennsylvania calls the field 'the scientific study of the strengths that enable individuals and communities to thrive.' One of the Center's webpages at the university is titled 'Authentic Happiness,' which I assume is in contradistinction to non-authentic happiness. They offer questionnaires on Authentic Happiness (yes, they write it with capitalization as if copyrighted) that they claim will measure 'character strengths and different aspects of happiness and well-being.' On the same webpage they also encourage visitors to 'Take a Facebook quiz to get your personal depression score and a set of depression-related words you use in your social-media status updates.' I was intrigued by this and wondered what would be my own 'personal depression score.' Unfortunately, I was not intrigued enough and decided to close the webpage before I actually did become depressed.

Now, don't get me wrong; I am all for happiness and positive well-being. I say 'No' to the specters of depression when they try to come sneaking into my house. Yet there is something that sits oddly here, and I think it has something to do with what was discussed earlier in the book; namely, the act of quantifying. The world of the pop spirit may be wildly ungovernable on one hand, yet the other hand is capturing it as a scientific study, in a questionnaire, and on a score card. The modern apparatus is taking the essential joy of happiness and packaging it as a skill to be acquired and paid for in the marketplace. Such 'positive acquisitions' may actually serve to diminish our genuine awareness and inner strengths. Positive Psychology (again capitalized) also has the in-built capacity to be a form of attractive self-deception that offers strategies that condition people to particular stimuli. The danger here is that whilst learning how to be happy we may end up diminishing our openness to genuine experiences and ranges of emotion. We may also become accustomed to a less authentic level of positivity which then blocks our capacity to evolve to higher states. By being delivered a positive mind we are in danger of giving over the effort to others and relinquishing our own responsibility. There is an insistence on harmony within Positive Psychology that veers very close to issues of self-censorship. We must ask ourselves whether such notions of harmony are ingenuous when corporate team slogans include, 'Winning by engaging the hearts and minds of every team member,' and 'I promise to make every experience outstanding.' What happens to a person's self-esteem when they realize that they haven't made every experience outstanding? Will they feel a failure? Remember, do we 'learn to fail or fail to learn?'

The pressure to harmonize might easily morph into a tyranny when pushed to the extreme. Positive Psychology, as a commercially packaged commodity, may actually add to the sense of hyperreality by replacing genuine relations and self-knowledge with a vision of corporate score cards. Is 'Authentic Happiness' then the real thing, as in genuine, natural authentic happiness, we wonder? As one commentator says,

> Positive psychology, like celebrity culture, the relentless drive to consume, and the diversionary appeals of mass entertainment, feeds off the unhappiness that comes from isolation and the loss of community. The corporate teaching that we can find happiness through conformity to corporate culture is a cruel trick, for it is corporate culture that stokes and feeds the great malaise and disconnect of the culture of illusion.[2]

The resurrection of novel, intriguing, and peripheral ideologies and trends in the online world has brought about a new celebration of 'consumer curiosities' that range from acquired happiness, sexual fetishes, to extra-terrestrials. With previous restraints of access now thawed out we are seeing a reappearance of these various spectacles that are being celebrated in whatever form online surfers desire. And desire, it seems, is highly sought after.

The Simulation of Desire

Seduction can also be interpreted as the art of manipulating our desires and the allure of deception. There is no doubt that modern life, and its institutions, attempt to seduce us. We are speeding faster on the outside whilst going almost nowhere within. We are breaking down as well as digitizing our boundaries of longing. Modern cultural landscapes and digital realms are de-territorializing the reach of the voyeur. There is now a shift in how desires are being redirected into new stimulated sensibilities and customized indulgences. We are being drawn into new modes of seduction – a form of 'always available' easy access. Seductions no longer tease us with waiting but can be instantaneously 'streamed' in the ever-present now. We are entering saturation point of the sexually explicit - online pornography raises its head as the new 'desire of despair' at the same time as children are being groomed, pedophiles are virtually gathering, and the beast within us licks its hideous lips.

Our modern cultures are more highly sexualized than ever as pornography has gone mainstream. Our advertising allures us with sexual imagery, references, and innuendoes. We are getting turned on from music videos that are filling up with scantily clad and booty-shaking extras that gyrate to the groove. Porn stars are making cameos in music videos and porn scenes are pantomimed and mimicked across the wide cultural scene. Fitness clubs offer pole-dancing and strip classes, and porn star memoirs are sold by top publishers and given table space in the big corporate bookshops. The once-peripheral world of pornography has now fused with the commercial mainstream. The moral bankruptcy of porn now shapes much of our western popular culture. As of 2008 there were an estimated 4.2 million porn sites on the public web (not to mention the infamous dark web), that were providing access to 72 million worldwide visitors monthly'[3] We can only guess how those figures have skyrocketed in the intervening years. Sex has always been big business. Sex sells better than bearded gurus and pop spirit combined. And many people see sex as a ticket to fame.

Sex tapes are famously 'leaked' online in a new twisted route to celebrity cultdom. These private performances are 'accidentally' made public in a bid for publicity and fame that represents a new and odd kind of fetishism, soaked in libidinal online viral flows. The simulation of desire is central to the digital realms, where arousal, demand, and creation co-exist. Almost any desires can be downloaded for instant gratification and viewer deflowering. Online pornography is a form of virus that absorbs endless amounts of libidinal energy that greases the cogs of digitized desire. These desires are soon to be projected into 'false bodies' as the robot sex toy becomes the next must-have gadget. Soon, Barbie will seem, well – quite timid. A recent report from futurologist Dr. Ian Pearson predicts that:

> By 2030, most people will have some form of virtual sex as casually as they browse porn today.
>
> By 2035 the majority of people will own sex toys that interact with virtual reality sex.
>
> We will start to see some forms of robot sex appearing in high-income, very wealthy households as soon as 2025.
>
> We will start to see robot sex overtaking human-human in 2050.[4]

Suddenly those closet-hidden doll inflatables will look like relics from the past. The experience of desire will soon be mediatized in a totally new way, with virtual reality and robot sex becoming a new and crowded playground. Yet this new experience is also likely to lead to an over-abundance of quick desire that may ultimately leave us unfulfilled - possibly leading to not sexual repression but rather a form of sexual depression. An over-plentiful supply of substitute sex may create a real wound of longing that a hyperreal world will be incapable, and unqualified, to cater for. With all the new banging may also come a few unexpected whimpers.

Bangs and Whimpers

The Tao Te Ching's nothingness is in danger of becoming the new pop spirit 'no-thing' as we step our way through the bardo years. We are also moving through a time of incredible visualization where the image is becoming dominant once again over literate culture. Our contemporary digital-media environs are like a self-reflexive sphere that projects back to us our desires and fears. This is similar to what was depicted in a science-fiction story by Stanislaw Lem called 'Solaris,' which was later hypnotically filmed by Andrei Tarkovsky. In Lem's story, the protagonists of a research space station are investigating an alien intelligence that is the oceanic sentient planet of Solaris. However, the sentient planet is in turn probing into the minds of the human researchers and investigating them. The planet responds by materializing thoughts, memories, and desires that are deep within the human mind. In this way each scientist is forced to confront those aspects that they have mentally hidden away. By encountering an unknown and alien entity, human thoughts, emotions, and desires become projected into a material reality. The sentient ocean of Solaris could be taken as a metaphor for our current hyperreal bardo world that seems to be doing a similar kind of reflection-projection. As the saying goes – be careful what you wish for, as you may end up getting it!

The first thing that a commodity culture does is to produce various forms of 'play.' Hence, many technologically-inspired innovations now emerging are creating a demand for simulated desires. Whether we wish for sexually-saturated media, immersive game-play with virtual head-sets, or robotic sex toys – everything in a bardo realm can at some point be manifested. We are like children at play with our toys, wishing for ever more elaborate satisfactions. We have the capacity to manifest our inner thoughts, desires, wishes; this is what we have always done through our inventions and creative imaginations. Yet in recent times it almost seems as if the boundary between wishes and their manifestation is thinning. It is likely that the new technological wave is facilitating and accelerating this phenomenon. And so, we really must be careful what we wish for, because there is a good likelihood that it will come about, in one way or another. Which makes us ask the obvious – why don't we wish for human betterment? After all, is it not the human imperative to strive and struggle to go beyond our present stage of development? Now more than ever, as our automated environments and artificially intelligent infrastructures organize our lives, we need to reach within us for the essential human.

The spirit that dwells within us, that makes us a soulful species, is far away from the popular spirituality that invades our news feeds and social media. It is not a collection of colorful pixels or groovy 10-minute videos. I'm positive about the great future awaiting us all once we cross these bardo times. It's going to be a spectacular future – but we have to get there first. And getting there entails moving beyond the immaturity of our commoditized desires.

The mass production of simulated desire also creates its contrary – the mass production of discontent and anxiety. And this too is subject to a media-stylized frenzy that breeds suicidal notions and terrorized fears. In our societies there exists a rampant psychopathology that creates and feeds on despair, aggression, and fear. As we cross the bardo we are compelled to fraternize with our fears.

A Bardo Chat with: Momus, Greek god of satire and mockery

Author (A): Hello there. I believe I am speaking with Momus?

Momus (M): Howdy to you there! You sure are; Momus is here, loud and clear. As for the rest of what you believe - I can't help you with that!

A: Ah, good. Thank you for agreeing to have a little chat.

M: No problem, buddy. I'm always up for a chat, and my tongue is as sharp as ever. That's what got me thrown out from keeping godly company. I guess they didn't like the hard truths! (laughs)

A: I guess not. And I also sense that you see clearly the strangeness of human society?

M: Aye, you could say that. Or, rather than saying strangeness, which is typically a human understatement, I'd say I see the unfairness, the oppression, the stupidity, and every other nook and cranny that runs through your games. You have the unenviable ability to amuse yourselves to death. Well, if that's how you want to play it! (whistles)

A: Well, I'm not sure if that's exactly how we want to play it, as you say. On the whole, most of us prefer to go down the road of progress with values, ethics, and dignity.

M: (sound of hands clapping) Bravo, you play your part well. Please, take a bow!

A: Come on, I don't mean like that.

M: Then don't come across all pompous like.

A: I didn't think I was.

M: Then start thinking! It doesn't matter what you say; you have over six thousand living languages and they're all just a bunch of words. Words are just fragments that can't tell a story properly. How are you going to find your inheritance if you're still fumbling with words? Action, my good man – action!

A: Yes, of course, there needs to be action.

M: Arrh, don't bore me! You're just throwing words back in my face. Do I look like I'm urinating in the wind? Come on, you, get with it! I mean humans can only be taken seriously through their actions. It doesn't matter what they say or what they write – it's what they do that really counts. You have to judge a person by their actions, and not their gabble.

A: Yes, that's right.

M: So damn right, it is! (laughs). Most of you lot down there say one thing and then do another. It drives me mad. I've been trying to figure it out for centuries. I even got to the point where my brain began to hurt – imagine that, buddy?! And now I think I have the answer, although it's not a very profound one.

A: And what is that?

M: It is simply that you're not aware you're doing it – for most of the time anyway. You actually believe that what you say is the same as what you do. You completely lack awareness in this matter. It's like you have a blind spot; or some blockage within you that simply refuses to see it.

What you lack as a species is awareness. Hey there – get aware. Wake up!

A: And how does one wake up?

M: (laughs and sound of hands clapping) How 'does one'...does one? What goes with you man, did you suddenly swallow a delusional pill that made you think you were a king? What's with this royal 'one'? You see what I'm saying – you're so attached to your words that you dress up in them like royalty.

A: (laughing) Okay then, how do we wake up? Come on, give it to me straight.

M: What do you expect – that I'm going to give it to you bendy? You have to wake up; you've got to crack some eggs and dance with the chickens. Nobody's going to do it for you. Stop being lazy and start being smart. Great things are expected from you lot. Don't keep us hanging around. There's a large company of us waiting on you guys.

A: What do you mean by waiting on us?

M: What, you think you're alone there? Well, I guess you do. First you run with the gods and then you dump them. You act as if you can do anything. You think you're living in a vacuum where nothing else matters. I sometimes roll in laughter watching you all strut about with your heads high. You want to know why there's strangeness in your societies? Well, that's you! You're the only strange things on this planet. Everything else fits in perfectly. Everything else has a place. Now you guys, you're lumbering about without a clue. That's why I'm so busy. It's your manifestations that gives me things to mock. What I satirize is yourselves. That's part of why I'm here. You needed someone, or something, to show these things back to you.

A: So it all comes back to us then. We are the laughing stock?

M: If you want to put it that way. But don't get all pitying about this. It's all a good thing – in the end, anyway. You are sometimes the laughing stock, other times the wayshowers and the light-bearers. You can be all these things. But it's the pompous stuff that really sets you back.

A: Our self-importance you mean?

M: Righty so. And all of the arrogance that comes with it. Why do you have to act this way? In every age you wear the dress that matches your attitudes. Watch this in you. See how you dress. And in these clothes you dress up in your personalities also. It's like you're going to a big ball, pompously strutting around trying to impress others. Why can't you just chill. Know that everything is here for you as you are. Everything in the world supports you. All of Nature and all the beings in your world – they want you to find yourselves too. They want to help. But you're all blind.

A: That's what I mean. I want to know how we can wake up from this blindness. I don't want it any more than you.

M: Then stop taking yourselves so seriously! Step back and step down. Like yourself and like others. And always do your best without hurting others. Life is not a race – it's a walking path. Walk on it, but not like a peacock! Walk like a human being. Grateful and humble. Otherwise you're going to receive some serious mocking from me!

A: Okay, got it – thanks! So, anymore advice?

M: Sure. Get moving and stop waffling. And that's on the house!

A: (laughs) Thanks, Momus.

M: No worries. Anyway, got to run. Nice chatting with you, although you weren't the smartest cookie. Ciao…

A: Cheers for that.

Endnotes

[1] Shah, I. 1985. *The Exploits of the Incomparable Mulla Nasrudin*. London: Octagon Press, p9.

[2] Hedges, Chris. 2010. *Empire of Illusion: The End of Literacy and the Triumph of Spectacle*. New York: Nation Books, p137-8.

[3] Hedges, Chris. 2010. *Empire of Illusion: The End of Literacy and the Triumph of Spectacle*. New York: Nation Books, p79.

[4] 'By 2050, human-on-robot sex will be more common than human-on-human sex, says report,' The Telegraph, http://www.telegraph.co.uk/technology/news/11898241/By-2050-human-on-robot-sex-will-be-more-common-than-human-on-human-sex-says-report.html, 29th September 2015 (accessed 20th June 2017)

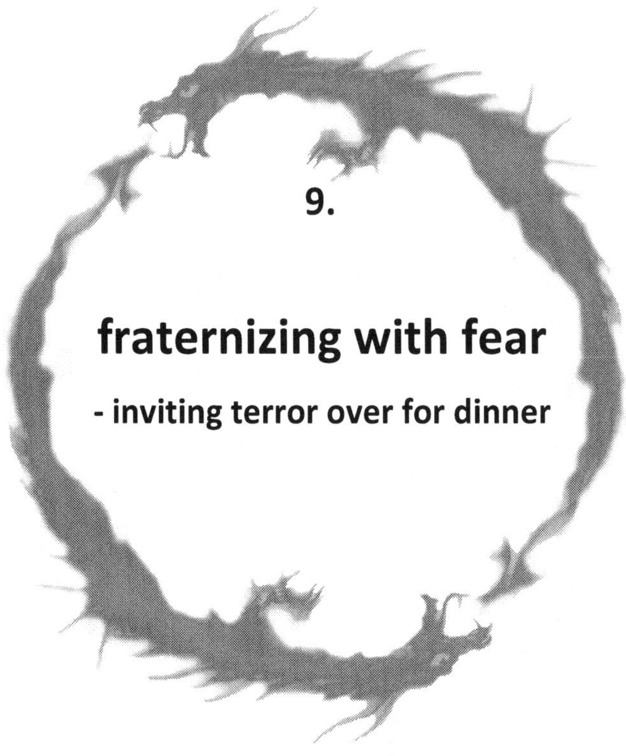

9.

fraternizing with fear

- inviting terror over for dinner

9. fraternizing with fear – inviting terror over for dinner

fɪə/

noun

an unpleasant emotion caused by the threat of danger, pain, or harm

Panic has now become something mystical

Paul Virilio

Panic on the streets of London
Panic on the streets of Birmingham
I wonder to myself
Could life ever be sane again?

The Smiths – 'Panic'

The end of the world is on everybody's mind, or so it seems. The wild catastrophic we see erupting across the globe and which is mirrored in our movies and entertainment comes from a part of us that senses things are out of kilter. It comes from a feeling that we are a part of something much larger than us, and maybe, just maybe, this larger collective is out of our singular control. The more the world has opened up through our global technologies the more it seems that the world is inextricably complex. As individuals we have never had to observe the world in this way before. We have never previously been faced with the prospect of a planetary civilization, although some past empires did come close. And into this mix come all the organizations, communities, associations, NGOs, and everyday people joining the global gathering and trying to make a difference for the better. And there are also those, in the minority, who are attempting to disrupt the flow.

For our ancestors, or even as recent as our grandparents or our parents, the world was always a very small place. It was our village, our town, our local communities. Problems were generally local issues that everyone knew about and which everyone either talked about, gossiped, or helped to solve. These were the 'conversations over the garden fence' type of thing, and stories were shared and laughed about in the local pub or parks. Yet now the local environment for the young people of the world *is* the world, and their stories are global stories.

When the Mayan culture issued their calendar several centuries ago depicting the end of a cycle, the whole world of today resonated with its shock waves. Luckily, and almost obviously, the world did not end, vaporize, or dematerialize into another dimension at the end of 2012. But it did show that ideas and fears can be spread in today's world faster than a contagious disease. And now, it appears, the end of the world is back on many peoples' minds. And the human mind is a greatly exploitable channel, or tool. Naturally, it is a great asset not only for us but also for others who wish to exploit its vulnerabilities. And an open mind can be an open vulnerability, which is an almost perfect opportunity. The images and stories that are fed to us become as food, whether they be a nutrient or a poison.

Fear as a New Best Friend

Fear used to be the exception, the anomaly, the bogey-man if you like. It was the evil, head-spinning possessed child of pea-green vomit that the church didn't want you to speak about. We steered away from talking about it; we hid behind the sofa or under the bed until it went away. And then we slipped out of our hiding places and told no-one about it; we didn't admit our fears to others and often not even to ourselves. Sometimes fear would come to us in dark, desperate moments and help shift us into survival mode for those necessary 'flight or fight' instants, which we would later be thankful for. Yet still we would refrain from sharing such sweat and heartbeat moments. Now that we have been propelled into the bardo times of hyperreality, fear has become our begrudging best friend. It has infiltrated into our lives like an unwanted stray that refuses to go away, and so we resentfully feed it until it sleeps on our doorstep and becomes an addition to the family. Many of us now live with fear in the house, and it has more than four furry legs. This fear has now taken on a double role – it both provides for our security as well as serving us our insecurities. It is a clever dude indeed.

If fear is all around us then maybe, we tell ourselves, the best way to combat this constant fear is to be ever battle-ready. You see, our reasoning has already been infiltrated and corrupted. And so, to live in constant fear requires that we learn how to manage it and to get along with our incongruous bed-fellow. We have very subtlety, almost without realizing it, established our own administration of fear, as philosopher Paul Virilio calls it. And once it is named it is one step closer to being institutionalized, which means becoming a part of our social politics and the systems that manage our lives.

The sense of fear and terror that has seeped into our own modern 'freedom-loving' lives has given consent for a 'security of terror' to be imposed upon us and to tyrannize us from within. The erosion of dualities and distinctions (as discussed previously) results in the breakdown of Friend vs. Enemy. A family member may potentially be an 'enemy terrorist,' or harboring 'terrorist tendencies' or downloading prohibited videos making them a 'person of suspicion.' Maybe a friend has recently changed their routine, is behaving oddly, or walking differently. In the past we may have considered this person to be in love or something similar – now they may be reported for being suspicious. This is the tyranny of terror that has erupted and is being pushed and thrust into our daily lives. This type of fear is infectious and spreads itself through all our centers and peripheries. It virtualizes itself into a vague yet deadly unknown enemy. We are being mauled by our own thought forms. We are being kindly reminded of the lurking 'high alert' levels by our own friendly governments.

Forms of national and global power are being deliberately manipulative in creating an *epidemic of consensus* amongst the masses. It is a new form of power that blackmails us through its very invisibility. Evil, and its attendant fear, has gone from being a solid, opaque form/ entity to now being a fluid, non-visible and illusive form of virus that flows through our societies in its various guises: terror, pandemics, digital harassment, corruption, blatant exploitation and manipulation, and so on. It is a virulent corruptive and corrosive presence that irradiates and contaminates. It is the radiation of evil that moves swiftly amongst our societies, virtually undetected. It is a dark worm that traverses our networks, our connections, our hubs – through the dark web - and influences the fluidity of modern life. There is also a fear-based 'fifth column' element to our so-called 'civilized' societies.

The 'fifth column' is a term coined during the Spanish Civil War and refers to individuals operating clandestinely within a larger body, such as a city or a country, in order to undermine it or attack it from within, often by mobilizing to assist an external attack. They may already be amongst us and yet we know them not. They are the secret saboteurs, the entrenched traitors. Does this sound familiar? We have been put on a constant state of alert, of watchfulness, of authorized paranoia. Our schoolchildren are asked to rat – sorry, to report – on any *potential* terrorist.

> Sir, the kid squatting next to me on the floor is sharpening his coloring crayon and giving me an odd look. He's a terrorist, Sir, and I think we should report him and get him carried off by the wardens. What - he was only constipated? But I thought it was a look of deviant terror he had in his eyes - how was I to know?

Exactly – how are we to know? One of the ever-present distortions of thinking in these bardo times is that violence resolves issues. And within a hyperreal realm this violence is taken to extremes, to the point where it becomes pure insanity, perpetrated through a reckoning of madness and despair. In an environment of manipulated fear, the most important strategy is to infiltrate our minds.

Previously in our societies fear was exercised through both actual and potential attack on the human body. It was a corporeal fear branded into flesh. Insurgents, enemies of the state – thieves and bread stealers – were put in chains and tied to posts in the main square with a sign around their neck upon which was written 'This is what happens to those who steal from kings.' Or they would be literally left hung out to dry for every passer-by to witness the power that the state/ monarchy had over every single individual body in their kingdom. The visual and the visceral became the fear virus, and it was most effective. But then came a time when it was no longer efficient. Too many people with too many human rights – and with urban centers sprawling for many kilometers in all directions there was no single main square anymore. So, fear shifted tactics and moved from the body to the mind. And it started to enter most effectively in the 20th century through those square devices that everyone had in their homes. Propaganda became the new tool for the administration of fear. We are not only the receivers of the fear virus but, more importantly, we are the consumers. There's a difference between putting a morsel of food in your mouth and chewing on it. We're chewing every piece of propaganda now like its fruit-flavored bubble-gum.

Panic is now in our governments as well as on our streets. There are those leaders rushing to close our borders, ship out strangers, and construct walls ever higher, at someone else's expense. It seems as if we have made terror our new best friend. And the other definition of terror is the informal one; of the person, especially a child, that causes trouble or annoyance – oh, he's a little terror! Well, that may sound like an apt description for humanity right now – an annoying child, scrapping in its own backyard and pulling the wings off flies, inflating frogs, and tormenting neighborhood animals. We are terror-inducing and terror-inflicted, and we've become so nervous that Chesterfield manufacturers cannot make their sofas fast enough for psychiatrists' offices. I guess a little fear is all you need. The incomparable Mulla Nasruddin comes to mind once again here -

> 'I'll have you hanged,' said a cruel and ignorant king, who had heard of Nasruddin's powers, 'if you don't prove that you are a mystic.'
> 'I see strange things,' said Nasruddin at once; 'a golden bird in the sky, demons under the earth.'
> 'How can you see through solid objects? How can you see far into the sky?'
> 'Fear is all you need.' smiled Nasruddin.[1]

Such fear that informs our societies today arises from a falsely-implanted perspective that, like a cancer, tricks the other cells into thinking it is one of their own. This fear does not belong to us – it is not *of us*. Yet it is certainly being manufactured *for us*.

Manufactured Fears

There is something going on right now in these bardo times that is insidious, and this something is causing fear

– whether it is fear of terrorism, of financial collapse, climatic upheaval, disease, *otherness*, or apathy. We are fraternizing with fear and allowing it to be woven into our lives. Through this it becomes our fear, and then we feed it, often drop by drop, until one day it grows too big for us. Genuine fear is raw; it is organic, meaning it is not made up. It's a primeval energy that puts into motion biological and chemical forces that establish a survival mode. Yet the fear that has infiltrated our societies today is just as lethal, yet it is unnatural. It is a constructed, manufactured fear that imposes particular degrees of power, at the individual, community, and state level. It is administered and managed and cleverly inserted into our high-visual and information-rich lives. It doesn't come about by accident but by calculated design. It is a virus of control that seemingly stems from a placeless, origin-less center. It is both peripheral and at the core – it exists everywhere and operates in an osmosis-like manner.

Philosopher Jean Baudrillard defines three types of catastrophes: natural, *manufactured* catastrophe (imminent and foreseeable), and *pre-programmed* catastrophe (deliberate and experimental). He notes how 'All the media live off the presumption of catastrophe and of the succulent imminence of death.'[2] Heavily mediatized images of war are used as propaganda – or what Baudrillard refers to as *information as catastrophe.* Living in highly visual cultures we are increasingly relying on the image and yet the image is indifferent, open and passive to abuse and photoshopping. We are the consumers of catastrophe in a hyperreality which is now uncertain and paradoxical. We are pursued by the morbid proclamations of being at risk from Weapons of Mass Destruction from Iraq, Libya, Iran, Syria, North Korea, and the rest of the 'Evil Gang' conveniently named by the Freedom Loving West. Fear and terror are now a marketable commodity, and we are its targeted consumers.

One of the aspects of living in a hyperreality is that it distorts the relationships between things, and this includes relations of risk. You could be killed crossing the road or sitting in a café or at a music concert, or in your office drawing cartoons, or in a school classroom. Similarly, someone pressing buttons could wipe out your credit rating, put out an immigration alert on you, or steal your digital identity. A punch in the face from a neighbor or someone in your local bar is the old, basic animal fear that came from a broad series of knowns. When fear or foe is known then it can be resisted by strength, force, courage, conflict, or negotiation. Yet in today's world our fears come from the unknowns that circulate through our increasingly high-velocity lives. And some of them are disguised as zeros and ones. Physical strength has no fixed or known place in a reality where the contagion is ethereal and elusive, albeit all the more devastating. Confrontation has been replaced by asymmetrical unease.

Conflict in our modern lives is no longer linear – Friend vs. Foe – but is incongruous, and this is deeply disturbing. It gives us great unease, and this uneasiness keeps us easier to control with promises of security and safety. All the rituals of airport security are not so much about catching the bomb-wielding terrorist but rather about training us all in fearful obedience. It is an unease that is generated to intentionally intervene and interfere with the 'reality' of our everyday lives.

The bottom line is that terror, as we now know it, is both asymmetrical and synchronized. It is asymmetrical in that it follows no linear or regular pattern; and it is synchronized in that thanks to global technologies of communication terror news can be shared simultaneously around the world affecting us emotionally like never before. Emotional impacts can now be synchronized globally, and this creates the possibility for a collective disturbance of human feelings on an unprecedented level. It is literally playing with fire – the fire of human fear, anger, and nervous energy. The specter of terror can also be synchronized through the *live feed*, having it streamed into our private spaces in real-time. In this sense, terror now possesses the power to pollute our personal and private spaces in a way not possible before. We now share a communal engagement with catastrophe – another way to put it is that we are now collectively *catastrophized* as a community. It is not just our 'personal terror' we are experiencing but the 'anonymous terror' that is inflicted asymmetrically upon targets that are unknown to us - and yet just as easily could be us. This is unnerving, and it makes us slightly paranoid.

Authorized Paranoia

When does fear end and paranoia begin? Much of the fear we feel today comes from a non-definable origin; that is, we know it exists but not from where it may come. This often results in this 'placeless fear' being internalized and then projected out into our societies and communities, creating an intangible anxiety and disquiet that is unnerving. In a high-velocity, hyperreal environment everything gets easily blown out of proportion. We are likely to end up creating our own environment of uneasiness. This is eerie, and again feeds into the sense of haunted lives that was mentioned at the beginning of this book. And when eeriness leads to anguish then we need to be concerned, as anguish creates stress, and many people are already stressed enough. Suicide is almost a pandemic in some countries, and it continues to be popular. The sharing of collective emotions also opens the way to a heightening of collective unease and panic – a nervousness on a mass scale, which must be avoided at all costs. We don't all want to catch a cold when only a few people sneeze. Well, no one ever said that experiencing these bardo times was going to be like taking a stroll by the river. At the very least, it is about maintaining our sanity.

In a world of increasingly compressed time, space, and speed, life is sure to feel like being inside a collective bubble. And it is this bubble that comes to define the general limits of our perceptions. Under normal, sane circumstances we should want to fill this bubble with oxygen, with an environment that nourishes us and helps us to grow. Yet instead we are allowing an environment of the eerie, of unease and nervousness, to fill up this bubble we are all breathing from. And life in this bubble is making us jump at every little thing. There is a popular saying – 'Fear is the deadliest assassin; it does not kill, but it keeps you from living.' Fear does a very good job of establishing a psychological tyranny.

Fear and terror - the potential presence of evil - is not only about physical suffering and pain. It is also the diabolical, the negative, the reversibility of sense, and the nonsensical nature of things out-of-their-place. And this topsy-turvy situation is depicted and often promoted by mainstream media channels. Such evils are an inversion of natural laws; an inversion of those inherent ideals of genuine welfare and betterment. Evil is a representation of an inhumane dimension. Yet the topsy-turvy nature of our hyperreal world is desensitizing us to such things. The nonsensical nature of modern life is now infiltrating into our very homes. An example of this is the recent Wikileaks release (March 2017) of 8,761 classified documents that showed how the CIA was using illicit hacking and surveillance strategies for gaining information unlawfully. One of these CIA programs, dubbed 'Weeping Angel,' was for hacking into Samsung Smart TVs to record conversations in our homes. This information would then be sent over the Internet, via the Smart TV, to a covert CIA server. This huge release of sensitive information – named as Vault 7 by Wikileaks – also indicated how not only televisions but also our smartphones and even anti-virus software are all vulnerable to CIA hacking.[1] And here is just one of the inversions of things in a hyperreal world. Not only are we being fed information and images of fear and terror to such an extreme where they are almost rendered banal, but our own TVs are spying on us. And yet this was just one revelation amongst many others, and the fuss soon seemed to die down. In other words, we just got used to it.

The desensitization through controlled media images and reports have taken us to a banality of tyranny whereby no one seems surprised anymore at the latest Wikileaks classified documents. This is the same whether it is the latest news about covert domestic spying, or collateral damage where scores of people are bombed at a wedding by a drone strike under the joystick control of an invisible hand in another country. Death, and unjust killings, has been rendered as aspects of the banality of evil that has ceased to move us in a way that such things once did. And this is affecting the very center of gravity of

1 For more information, see - https://www.theguardian.com/media/2017/mar/07/wikileaks-publishes-biggest-ever-leak-of-secret-cia-documents-hacking-surveillance

our cultures.

For many societies today, the center of gravity has shifted from social management to security. It would have been better to say that it was originally social welfare and well-being rather than social management that was the center of gravity, but this has rarely been the case in modern, especially industrial, societies. And now the need for security in a global world of increasing risks is a very real one in our hyperreal world. It is not only a question of authorized paranoia. It is a question of how states, authorities, and institutions instigate and exercise these securities. Fraternizing with our fears facilitates its own need for implementing greater security which in turn triggers greater unease and insecurity. States, cities, and societies declare their 'States of Emergency' with increasing frequency, allowing them to exercise non-constitutional powers that curb civil liberties, and the rest. Yet it is all legitimized through the promotion of unease and the threat – real and/or imagined – of terror arriving from unknown places, ethereal and asymmetrical. Pandora's box has been opened and those in authority seem to want to throw things at the box rather than trying to put the lid back on. The fear is lurking around, insidious and crafty, and it's making a lot of people uneasy and a little angry.

Anger is finding release in both traditional forms of violence as well as in the surreal and the absurd. People are attacked in the streets for no reason, or because the attacker didn't like someone's face, or because they were told to get off the bus or leave the bar. In many of our modern 'civilized' societies there has erupted an 'absurdum of anger,' which has resulted in meaningless deaths. People in the 'wrong place at the wrong time' have had their lives cut short for no discernible reason other than bad luck. There is a pathological strain of anger hanging murkily around some of our societies like smog. Even as far back as the early seventies Theodore Roszak asked,

> ...is it merely coincidence that, in the midst of so much technological mastery and economic abundance, our art and thought continue to project a nihilistic imagery unparalleled in human history?...It is not that our technological achievements are all worthless...It is rather that they are *meaningless* in the absence of a transcendent correspondence.[3]

And again, here we come to the point. And the point is that there is no real meaning in the absence of our possible transcendence or betterment.

There are forces prevalent in life that we are generally unaware of, and these forces use the medium of fear to impact us and to socially manage our thoughts and behavior. Often these forces escape our attention because they are not presented in standard ways, as solid objects or obvious causes. And yet our best defense and protection against the forces of fear, terror, and tyranny are to be aware of them first. Our protection against them is our knowing about them. If you know about them, you can be protected and guarded.

In these bardo times we need to be aware that there will be such forces striving to paralyze and make difficult our human development and progress. We are going to have to learn how to see things as they come - or even before they come. We have to be smart, aware, and alert. We have to have the discernment to know when something doesn't feel or seem right. In short, we need to know when someone, whether an individual or a group, is trying to manipulate or coerce us. Crossing these bardo years is not going to be a particularly smooth crossing, but it *is* about crossing. It's about getting there – arrival.

So far, I have discussed the insidious nature of the fear that we are fraternizing with in many of our cultures. Also, how this administration of fear is managed and, in the words of Baudrillard, is a form of both *manufactured* and *pre-programmed* catastrophe. Yet it is largely distinct from the primal and organic fear that we have evolved with over millennia. As such, it is unnatural to us, and does not sit well with our essential natures. To counteract this creeping fear, we need to recognize it for what it is. The first step is to be aware of its presence as it weaves through our modern lives. The next step is to not give it permission to impact us. We need to live with the *real*, and not with the negative, the reversibility of sense, and the nonsensical nature of things out-of-their-place. We need to get our internal house in order during these bardo years so that when we come out at the other side we'll be sane and grounded enough to move on swiftly and wisely. First, we need to resist the mechanical sleep that is creeping into our souls in these bardo times. Beware the automated lives of the hyperreal!

A Bardo Chat with: Eris, Greek goddess of strife and discord

Author (A): Hello…Eris? …Eris?

Eris (E): Whoa, is that you there?

A: Yes, I think so.

E: You sound hesitant.

A: I'm speaking with Eris, the goddess of strife and discord. Should I be hesitant?

E: Sure – be hesitant; very hesitant! (laughs). No, you'll be fine; I'm not here to cause any more wars.

A: Ah yes, the famous Troy affair and the golden apple of discord. Well, let's not get started on that.

E: Yeah, let's not even go there! (giggles). So, what's on your mind then?

A: I've been thinking recently about all the strife and discord that seems to be entering the world in recent years. I know these things have always been around, but it just seems like there is more discord than normal. I hope you've got nothing to do with all this?

E: Not likely! Besides, you don't need me around to help you; you're doing just fine creating your own discord. I'm happy to sit back and watch it unfold.

A: Lucky you – but down here things seem kind of weird. You know, out of kilter. And it's affecting people differently.

E: And how is it affecting you?

A: Well, I seem to be okay, thanks. As always, I'm trying to see things in perspective, and not to get pulled into the mess. A lot of it appears to be manufactured to me.

E: Well, it is and it isn't. But you're right about trying to maintain perspective. Strife has always been around; it is part of the tug and pull of life. In fact, ironic as it sounds, strife is often needed before harmony and coherence.

A: How's that?

E: It's quite simple. The cosmos as you know it is forever being pulled toward greater coherence. Yet discord is a prime driver in this. This is natural discord which exists for order to come about – if you get my meaning?

A: Sure, I can understand that order comes out of chaos, as they say. So, some strife is necessary. But that's natural discord, isn't it?

E: Yes, it is natural in that it is part of the underlying laws of your reality and the cosmos reflects this. Of course, we must be clear here. When I talk about 'natural' I am referring to what are the laws governing your realm. These are not 'natural' to us. Yet by knowing how the natural laws operate in your realm is useful. It helps to see things on a grander level, and to know that discord is not necessarily a bad thing. There are unsettlings, so to speak, so that things can come together later on. Think of it as planting. First you need to prepare the soil. Perhaps you need to plough it, to turn over the earth, before you can plant for the new season. There are energies, and cycles, that have this function. Some of your kind are aware of this, although mostly this goes unsuspected.

A: And what about the manufactured stuff?

E: Ah, well - that is your problem! (laughs). It's all about power. You've got some folks down there with you who don't want to let go of their power structures. They're the old guard and they're not happy about the incoming changes.

A: So, that means then that some good change is on its way?

E: Oh yeah, you've got some fun times ahead. But believe me kid, there's a few bumps coming your way first. But it's all energy - you're receiving some decent sized energy blasts in your realm.

A: And that's a good thing?

E: It will be eventually. However, again I have to say that it's difficult for us to use these terms of 'good' and 'bad.' How can you know what's good for you if you can't see further than your own nose, as you people like to say?

A: That's a good point. Again, I guess it's a relative thing.

E: Relative, yes, as all things are. And what might be useful for one person may damage the other. Discord and strife are occurrences that need to pass, in the larger scheme of things. And they will pass. Sometimes interventions are required for a little chaos to erupt in order to spur things into motion. That was where I often come into the picture.

A: The golden apple episode?

E: (laughs). Oh yeah, such as the golden apple. It's all part of the game, no matter how spontaneous it looks from smaller eyes. Anyway, for you my dears, there's going to be a few disruptive waves that will rock your boats as well as propelling you forward, which is their function. There's so much new stuff coming down the line. The problem is that there are a lot of mean people down there who don't want to accept the coming flows. As you say, they don't want to get off the line. But they're going to get pushed off. Whoosh!

A: In the meantime, the rest of us have to keep our balance.

E: You got it. Stay sane and don't get distracted by all the discord that's being pushed your way.

A: That's exactly what I say. Don't get taken in by the all the fear mongering.

E: Yes, there's going to be a lot of that. They're going to be throwing it all around the place - fear here, tyranny there. But these are the actions of desperate people. They're on the way out - and with strategies like that they need to be! War has been an active feature on your planet. Violence can be functioning or non-essential. There are times when warfare erupts on your planet due to influences that are beyond you. These are cosmic forces that you are largely unaware of. Let's just call them the friction of the planets. A bad energy washes over your planet and aggravates circumstances. What you refer to as warfare is both an aggravation as well as a cure for the aggravation. Again, hard to really explain this. Then there are the petty wars which many of your power-hungry personalities have started. And that is just childish.

A: Nothing like a classy golden apple to get a war started.

E: (laughs) Yes, that was classy of me, I do admit. Yet don't believe the history – or the hype! It actually was a required act that I accepted to fulfil. These are just some of the things that we folks have to do as service. I just got landed with the golden apple. But it could have been a lot worse. I mean, there have been worse! (laughs). But anyway kid, just hang on and don't get duped by the fear. Remember, you're better than that. Good luck with it all, and don't forget to smile once in a while. I'm off to make trouble over yonder! (laughs).

A: Thanks Eris!

Endnotes

[1] Shah, I. 1982. *The Sufis*. London: Octagon, p65.

[2] Baudrillard, Jean. 1994. *The Illusion of the End*. Cambridge: Polity Press, p55.

[3] Roszak, Theodore. 1972. *Where the Wasteland Ends: Politics and Transcendence in Postindustrial Society*. New York: Doubleday & Company, p379.

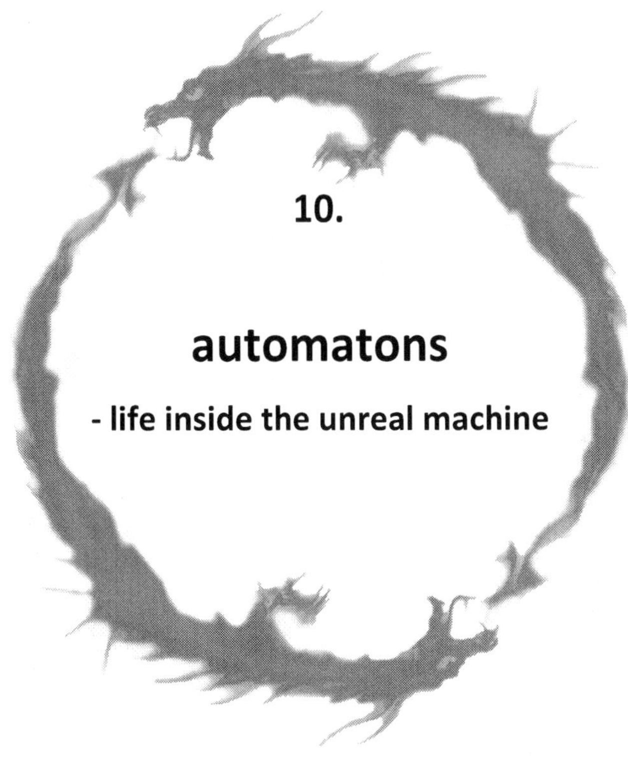

10.

automatons

- life inside the unreal machine

10. automatons – life inside the unreal machine

ɔːˈtɒmət(ə)n/

noun

a moving mechanical device made in imitation of a human being.
a machine which performs a range of functions according to a predetermined set of coded instructions.
used in similes and comparisons to refer to a person who seems to act in a mechanical or unemotional way.

"Don't you wish you were free, Lenina?"
"I don't know what you mean. I am free. Free to have the most wonderful time. Everybody's happy nowadays."
He laughed. "Yes, 'Everybody's happy nowadays.' We have been giving the children that at five. But wouldn't you like to be free to be happy in some other way, Lenina? In your own way, for example; not in everybody else's way."
"I don't know what you mean," she repeated.

Aldous Huxley, *Brave New World*

Are we turning into a mass of unaware sleepwalkers? Our eyes are seemingly open and yet we are living as if asleep and the dream becomes our waking lives. Or perhaps we have been sold our dreams as commodities just to keep us conveniently drugged. Soon we may quietly slip into a non-defined state where there is no difference between apparent action and indifference. Although open and gazing outwards, the eyes are of little use when the mind is unaware. This is the rampant unawareness that pervades the hyperreality that surrounds us. And the more this becomes 'hypernormalized,' the more we allow ourselves to be neutralized into a form of mental passivity. It is the simulation that eventually erases any ideas or ideologies that may contest its existence. Individual personal power is an anomaly, a glitch that the system tries to eradicate from the program. But these glitches are our very future. If indeed there is to be a future, then it cannot survive as a homogenous mass; it must be filled with human (and humane) glitches that share a common accord of well-being and betterment. We have to stay awake whilst in the bardo times. We have to know just where we are going and *how* we are getting there. That means we need to struggle to be awake and alert and to resist the loss of meaning. Sitting at home on our sofas munching popcorn, whilst watching the horde of zombies in *The Walking Dead*, has to be one of the grandest ironies of our times.

Welcome to the Living Dead

It seems that more and more people, in the highly technologized nations at least, are in danger of succumbing to the epidemic of uniformity. People follow cycles of fashions and wear stupid clothes when they think it is the 'in thing;' and hyper-budget films take marketing to a whole new level forcing parents to rush out to buy the merchandise because their kids are screaming for it. And if one child in the class doesn't have the latest toy like all their classmates then they are ostracized for this lack. Which means that poor mummy and daddy have to make sure they get their hands on these gadgets. Put the two items together – zombies and uniformity – and what do you get? Welcome to the phenomenon of Black Fridays, which have become the latest manifestation of national Zombie Days.

Unless you've been living in a cave somewhere (or living a normal, peaceful existence) then you will know what this event is – but let me remind you anyway of what a Black Friday is. It is a day when members of the public are infected with the 'must buy' and 'act like an idiot' virus that turns them into screaming, raging hordes banging on the doors of hyper-market retailers hours before they open. Many of these hordes sleep outside all night to get early entry. Then when the doors are finally opened they go rushing in fighting and screaming as if re-enacting a scene from *Games of Thrones*. Those that do survive the fisticuffs come away with trolleys full of boxes too big to carry. This display of cultural psychosis, generally named as idiocracy, is also a condition nurtured by societies based on high-consumption with even higher inequalities of wealth distribution. In other words, a culture conditioned to commodity accumulation will buy with fervour when things are cheap. This is because although conditioned to buy, they lack the financial means to satiate this desire. Many people suffer from a condition which psychologists have named as 'miswanting,' which means that we desire things we don't like and like things we don't desire. What this is really saying is that we tend to 'want badly' rather than having genuine need. What we are witnessing in these years is an epidemic of idiocracy and its propagating faster than post-war pregnancies. And yet we are programmed by our democratic societies to not think differently. In this respect, many people also suffer from a condition known as 'confirmation bias.'

Confirmation bias is our conditioned tendency to pick and choose that information which confirms our pre-existing beliefs or ideas. Two people may be able to look at the same evidence and yet they will interpret it according to how it fits into and validates their own thinking. That's why so many debates go nowhere as people generally don't wish to be deviated away from those ideas they have invested so much time and effort in upholding. It's too much of a shock to realize that what we thought was true, or valid, is not the case. To lose the safety and security of our ideas would be too much for many people. As the 13th century Persian poet Saadi put it – 'Deep in the sea are riches beyond compare. But if you seek safety, it is on the shore.' It is now well understood in psychology that we like to confirm our existing beliefs; after all, it makes us feel right!

Many of our online social media platforms are adhering to this principle by picking and choosing those items of news, events, etc that their algorithms have deemed we are most likely to want to see. Here we have the emergence of a potentially useful tool that if we are not careful may end up confirming our biases to us – the customization bubble mentioned earlier in the book. As convenient as it may seem, it is unlikely to be in our best interests in the long term.

The increasing automation of the world around us is set to establish a new ecology in our hyperreality. We will be forced to acknowledge that algorithms and intelligent software will soon, if it isn't already, be running nearly everything in our daily lives. Historian Yuval Harari believes that 'the twenty-first century will be dominated by algorithms. "Algorithm" is arguably the single most important concept in our world. If we want to understand our life and our future, we should make every effort to understand what an algorithm is.'[1] Algorithms already follow our shopping habits, recommend products for us, pattern recognize our online behavior, help us drive our cars, fly our planes, trade our economies, coordinate our public transport, organize our energy distribution, and a lot, lot more that we are just not really aware of. One of the signs of living in a hyperreality is that we are surrounded by an invisible coded environment, written in languages we don't understand. We are surrounded by what cultural historian Langdon Winner termed 'concealed electronic complexity' meaning that no connections are mundane, despite the feeling that we are increasingly living in an abstraction.

Abstracted Lives

Modern societies are adapting to universal computing infrastructures that will usher in new arrangements and relations. Of course, these are only the early years, although there is already a lot of uncertainty and unpredictability. As it is said, industrialization didn't turn us into machines and automation isn't going to turn us into automatons. Which is more or less correct; after all, being human is not *that* simple. Yet there will be new dependencies and relations forming as algorithms continue to create and establish what can be called 'pervasive assistance.' Again, it is a question of being alert so that we don't feel compelled just to give ourselves over to our algorithms. The last thing we want is for a bunch of psychologists trying to earn yet more money from a new disease of 'algorithmic dependency syndrome' or something similar.

It needs stating that by automating the world we also run the risk of being distanced from our own responsibilities. And this also implies, importantly, the responsibility we have to ourselves – to transcend our own limitations and to develop our human societies for the better. We should not forget that we are here to mature as a species and we should not allow the world of automation to distract us from this. Already literature and film have portrayed such possibilities. Examples are David Brin's science-fiction novel *Kiln People* (2002 – also adapted into the film *Surrogates*, 2009), which clearly showed how automation may provide a smokescreen for people to disappear behind their surrogate substitutes.

Algorithms are the new signals that code an unseen territory all around us. We are inundated in code that re-assembles us into digital identities. As an eerie warning to us on this, Facebook recently did a test on its own algorithm to see whether it was a better judge of human personalities than a person's own friends, parents, or spouse. The final result was that 'the algorithm needed a set of only ten Likes in order to outperform the predictions of work colleagues. It needed seventy Likes to outperform friends, 150 Likes to outperform family members and 300 Likes to outperform spouses. In other words, if you happen to have clicked 300 Likes on your Facebook account, the Facebook algorithm can predict your opinions and desires better than your husband or wife!'[2] In a world of rapidly increasing automation and digital identities we'll have to keep our wits about us in order to retain what little of our identities we have left. We want to make sure that we don't get lost in our emoji messages, our smilies of flirtation; or, even worse, loose our life in the 'death cult' of the selfies.

Identities by their very nature are constructs; in fact, we can go so far as to call them fake. They are constructed from layers of ongoing conditioning which a person identifies with. This identity functions as a filter to interpret incoming perceptions. The limited degree of perceptions available to us almost guarantees that identities fall into a knowable range of archetypes. We would be wise to remember that who we are is not always the same as what we project. And yet some people on social media are unable to distinguish their public image from their personal identity, which starts to sound a bit scary. Even Facebook's founder Mark Zuckerberg has said: 'The days of you having a different image for your work friends or co-workers and for the other people you know are probably coming to an end pretty quickly.'[3] Zuckerberg also mentioned that having two identities – in other words, offline and online - was an example of a lack of integrity. Oh dear, it now appears we have a crisis in identity ethics. Philosopher Jean Baudrillard, not opposed to saying what he thought, stated it in another way:

> We are in a social trance: vacant, withdrawn, lacking meaning in our own eyes. Abstracted, irresponsible, enervated. They have left us the optic nerve, but all the others have been disabled...All that is left is the mental screen of indifference, which matches the technical in-difference of the images.[4]

Baudrillard would probably be the first to agree that breathing is often a disguise to make us think that someone is alive. After all, don't we breathe automatically without thinking about it? It begs the question whether many of us are stepping through these bardo years in a social coma.

We must be wary of the mathematization of reality, where the quantitative replaces the qualitative as the measurement of human life. The digital life must not be about numbers but about the quality of immersion, interaction, and participatory engagement that enhances the quality of human life and not detracts from it. We must not make the human spirit obsolete just because our technological elites are dreaming of a trans-human future. Speaking of such futures, inventor and futurist Ray Kurzweil predicts that in the 2030s human brains will be able to connect to the cloud and to use it just like we use cloud computing today. That is, we will be able to transfer emails and photos directly from the cloud to our brain as well as backing up our thoughts and memories. How will this futuristic scenario be possible? Well, Kurzweil says that nanobots - tiny robots constructed from DNA strands – will be swimming around in our brains. And the result? According to Kurzweil we're going to be funnier, sexier, and better at expressing our loving sentiments. Well, that's okay then – nanobot my brain up! Not only will being connected to the computing cloud make us sexier and funnier humans, it will even take us closer to our gods says Kurzweil – 'So as we evolve, we become closer to God. Evolution is a spiritual process. There is beauty and love and creativity and intelligence in the world - it all comes from the neocortex. So we're going to expand the brain's neocortex and become more godlike.'[5] It's hard to argue with such a bargain – a few nanobots in our brain to become godlike? I can imagine a lot of people will be signing up for this. There may even be a hefty monthly charge for those wanting more than 15GB of back-up headspace. Personally, I prefer the headspace that's ad infinitum and priceless. I hope I'm not in the minority.

Looking at the choices on offer in our automated bardo world it seems that there is the zombie option, which comes with add-on idiocracy (basic model), and the trans-human nanobot sexy-god upgrade (pricy). But then let's not forget that in an automated world it may be the sentient robots that come out on top. Now, that would be an almost perfect demonstration of a simulation reality.

Life in Imitation

There are those who believe that self-awareness is going to be the end game of artificial intelligence – the explosive 'wow factor' that really throws everything into high gear. Does that mean there will be no further development of our own self-awareness as humans? Full human self-awareness - wouldn't that be a fine thing? The new trend now is deep machine-learning to the point where machines will program not only themselves but also other machines. Cognitive computer scientists are attempting to recapture the essence of human consciousness in the hope of back-engineering this complexity into machine code. It's a noble endeavor, if not at least for their persistence. The concern here is that if machines do finally achieve sentience then the next thing that we'll need to roll out will be machine psychologists. Consciousness, after all, comes at a price. There is no free lunch when it comes to possessing a wide-awake brain. With conscious awareness comes responsibilities, such as values, ethics, morality, compassion, forgiveness, empathy, goodness, and good old-fashioned love. And I personally like the love part (gives me a squishy feeling every time!).

It may not actually be the sentient robots we need to worry about; it's the mindless ones we need to be cautious of (of course, we could say the same thing about ourselves). One of the methods used in training such robots is, in the words of their trainers, to provide them with enough 'intrinsic motivation.'[1] Not only will this help the robots to learn their environments, it is also hoped that it will foster attention in them to acquire sufficient situational awareness. If I were to write a science-fiction scenario on this I would make it so that the sentient robots end up being more human than we are, and humans turn into their automated counterparts. Funny, maybe - but more so in the funny-bone hurting sort of way rather than the laugh-out-loud variety. Or perhaps it's already been done. It appears that we are attempting to imbue our devices with qualities we are also striving to possess for ourselves. Humans are naturally vulnerable; it is part of our organic make-up. Whatever we create may inherit those vulnerabilities. However, this here is not a

[1] For some discussion on this, see - https://futurism.com/what-will-the-rise-of-conscious-machines-mean-for-human-beings/

discussion on the pros and cons of smart machines and artificial intelligence (there are other more qualified books on that huge topic).

What I am saying is that we again have the magician's sleight-of-hand situation in that while we are watching the left hand we don't see what the right hand is doing. While we are creating, testing, worrying, or arguing over machines and their like we are taking our attention away from the center – ourselves. The trick of surviving in the 'unreal machine' of life is by becoming more human, the very antithesis of the robotic. Technology can assist us in interacting and participating to a better degree with our environments. The question, as always, is the uses to which such tools are put – and by whom. Such tools can help us realize our dreams, or they can entrap us in theirs. Algorithms, smart machines, intelligent infrastructure, and automated processes: these are all going to come about and be a part of our transforming world. And in many respects, they will make life more comfortable for us. Yet within this comfort zone we still need to strive and seek for our betterment. We should not allow an automated environment to deprive us of our responsibility, and need, to find meaning and significance in our world. Our technologies should force us to acknowledge our human qualities and to uplift them, and not to turn us into an imitation of them.

Another metaphor for the simulated 'robotic' creature is the golem. The golem legend speaks of a creature fashioned from clay, a Cabbalistic motif which has appeared frequently in literary and cinematic form. Despite the commoditized culture industry of cinema (especially in Hollywood) the cinematic vision has been used as a reflection, or meditation, on issues that run central through our lives. The Cabbalistic automaton that is the golem, which means 'unformed,' has often been used in cinema to show the struggle between mechanical limitation and human feelings. This struggle depicts the tension that combines cogs and consciousness; the entrapment in matter and the spirit of redemption and liberation. One of the most famous of the golem legends is the one associated with Rabbi Loew of seventeenth-century Prague who created his creature from clay mud of the local Vltava river to protect his people. Soon his very own creation grows in strength and threatens his creator, and so Rabbi Loew reverses his magic spell and returns the creature to dust. Frankenstein is a later western retelling of the golem myth. This is a myth that speaks of the hubris in humanity fashioning its own creatures and 'magically' bestowing life upon them. It is the act of creating a 'sacred machine' from the parts and pieces of a material world and then to imbue them with human traits. And through this human likeness they are required to fulfil human chores and work as slaves. Sounds familiar? The Cabbalistic humanoid – the sentient robot – is forever doomed, almost like the divine nature of Man trapped within the confines and limitations of a material reality. They represent the conflict of being torn between a fixed fate and freedom.

Cinematic explorations of this theme include *Blade Runner*, *Robocop*, *A.I.*, and *Bicentennial Man*, amongst many others. Both *Blade Runner* and *Robocop* depict a human world of violence and the need to create a sentient creature for protection and service; whilst *A.I.* and *Bicentennial Man* demonstrate the wish to create out of emotion and feelings. Running through all these cinematic portrayals is the clash of natures between the human and the non-human. In *Blade Runner* (1982) the major conflict is between Roy (the Replicant – played by Rutger Hauer) and Deckard (the one who hunts down rogue Replicants – played by Harrison Ford). Within this interplay there are constant questions raised as to what constitutes conscious life, as often the poles are turned showing the Replicants as more human than Deckard, the supposed human hunter. Finally, we are left with the ambiguous notion that Deckard might himself unknowingly be a Replicant, implanted with false memories. This idea mirrors the motif that we harbor a wish, a dream, to fashion something pure and yet the error is always that our human traits end up within our own creations. This reflects elements of the Cabbalistic belief in the urge to transcend corrupt matter through realizing the perfect human. And yet, as these films show, there are dangers in blurring the lines between human and automation. The final irony of course is that cinema itself may be yet another form of enslavement - of the viewer compelled to consume the glossy celluloid product. Our material reality may be the ultimate *unreal machine*. We are the cogs, the clay golem, the imperfect creature fashioned by another. Our fears of automation may only be a reflection of our own automation. We struggle to express some form of release whilst unaware that the binds that mechanize us are forever tightening.

We have now shifted through the zombie-idiocracy model (basic), the trans-human nanobot sexy-god model (pricy), to arrive at the realization that it is *us* – and not our sentient robots - that are likely to be the automaton (tragic). And this is the biblical fall from grace; the disconnection from our god(s). We have come loose from Central Source and we have lost our way.

These bardo times is the limbo period where we've hopped off one stage of the journey although we have yet to place ourselves onto another. One of the definitions of automation encountered at the beginning of this chapter is 'a machine which performs a range of functions according to a predetermined set of coded instructions.' In this bardo realm we are experiencing the upsurge of a coded environment, and it's giving out coded instructions aimed at programming our own functioning. This is the hyperreal realm where zombies, cyborgs, and golem robots all reside – but it is not the place for the genuine human. Things are going to have to change. Not only do we have to retain our humanity, we also must remain sane. With our continuing modern technologies, our augmented reality and bioengineering, the difference between fiction and reality will blur even further. And this blurring is likely to become more prominent as people increasingly try to reshape reality to fit around their own imaginative fictions. Staying sane, grounded, and balanced is going to be a very, very good option for the days to come.

Life is going to get trickier for a while, as we all squabble for space in the shared playroom. We are going to be sharing our planetary space with the new smart machines. I am reminded of the Dr. Seuss book *Horton Hears a Who!* that has the refrain, 'a person's a person no matter how small.' Size doesn't count – but being human does. And staying human in these bardo years will be the hard task allotted to us as the spaces around us increasingly techno-mutate into an enveloping digital environment. Welcome to the new psychosphere.

A Bardo Chat with: Ptah, Egyptian god of craftsmen

Author (A): Hello Ptah? Hello, are you there?

Ptah (P): I am (deep voice)

A: Ah, thank you. So, you are the god of craftsmen then?

P: I am indeed – of all the crafts: metalworking, sculpture, carpentry, construction. All craftsmen create, and I am the patron of creation.

A: Wonderful.

P: Why is that so? Are you a craftsman – one who creates?

A: Well, in a way. I try to create through the craft of words. I work a different way with my hands; but yes, I still create.

P: There are many ways to create. Some is through hardworking of the hands, and I have dealt much with these persons. I understand also there is creation through projection of thoughts and through transcribing. I have guided your craftsmen for many ages. You have capacity for invention, and for curiosity.

A: Yes, when we transcribe the ideas that come into our minds, it is like a craft. The word is itself a craft. We are only the carriers.

P: Ah yes, that is so.

A: And it's the curiosity which is our strength, and perhaps our weakness.

P: Your meaning?

A: There is a strong push now to move from craftsmen to creators. Our scientists are exploring bioengineering, creating new biological and hybrid organisms. And our computer scientists are attempting to create machine intelligence.

P: The cosmos is filled with intelligence. Why should you feel that you have the sole right to it?

A: I don't. I'm fully aware we are not the only species to manifest intelligence. What I'm wondering is whether we should be the ones to create another form of intelligence.

P: You yourselves were created. Do you not see a pattern?

A: Well, I wasn't talking about a god here.

P: Neither was I. There is creation and intelligence at all levels. Your whole planet is not only full with intelligence but is intelligence itself. Intelligence is universal. It is everything that is. There is nothing that is not intelligent. Why do you always harken back to your idea of gods?

A: Well, that's a good point because it brings up the issue of humans playing at being gods.

P: (low deep chuckle) Yes, you do like to play! But leave the gods out of this one. Creation, and the ability to create, is one of the wondrous aspects of your cosmos. You do not need to think of yourselves as gods to create. Do children building sandcastles think of themselves as gods?

A: Maybe not – but we are hardly talking about sandcastles here.

P: Yet you are building all the same. Let me tell you something – you do not create conscious intelligence. It already exists. You only create vessels to receive it. Let go of your arrogance and pride. You are not able to get within an inch of creating consciousness. Without the gift of the cosmos you yourselves are but machines, reacting to stimuli. You were given a gift. And you are not the ones to decide if and when that gift should be bestowed. Create - experiment! - and in doing so you will have the opportunity to understand your own humanity.

A: Good advice.

P: I'm not giving advice. I am not a counsellor. I speak what I know to be my truths - take them or leave them, as humans have always done.

A: I should speak with you more often.

P: Don't think so highly of yourself - I'm doing you a favor.

A: Right - got it.

P: Anything else? Your dimension is not conducive to me. Being here too long brings back arduous memories (low chuckle)

A: Oh, okay. I won't keep you much longer then; just a final question about technology. Are we doing the right thing in our continued development of smart technologies?

P: That question does not mean much to me. It tells me more about your own thinking, which is not yet of a high enough level to grasp the issues of which we can speak.

A: Mmm...okay. But could we give it a try?

P: Briefly. You speak of both technology and smart. These are concepts which are relative to your own time-space matrix. Technology is a term you overly misuse. In a sense, everything is a technology - including the human race.

You seem to think technology is just something metallic or artificial. I tell you now that all of life in your cosmos is a form of technology. Smart – this is such an obscure term it has no sense. You think people are smart because their brains can retain information. You wrongly define the sense you wish to convey here. I would suggest you consider this notion in terms of being closer or further from the Source. Smart is a social ranking system you have – it bears no relation to your conscious self. Finally, are you doing the right thing? Haven't you ever heard of free will? That's why we mostly leave your planet alone. Not the best of ideas, in my humble opinion. Well, that is all.

A: Well, thank you, Ptah. You have given me much to consider.

P: Perhaps you may now consider on how to ask more appropriate questions.

A: Yes, I will certainly work on that. Thank you.

P: I go.

A: Goodbye.

Endnotes

[1] Harari, Yuval Noah. 2017. *Homo Deus - A Brief History of Tomorrow*. London: Vintage, p97.

[2] Harari, Yuval Noah. 2017. *Homo Deus - A Brief History of Tomorrow*. London: Vintage, p396.

[3] Cited in Carr, Nicholas. 2015. *The Glass Cage: Where Automation is Taking Us*. New York: Bodley Head, p206.

[4] Baudrillard, Jean. 2008. *The Perfect Crime*. London: Verso, p144.

[5] Miles, Kathleen, 'Ray Kurzweil: In The 2030s, Nanobots In Our Brains Will Make Us 'Godlike'', Huffington Post, 10th January 2015, http://www.huffingtonpost.com/entry/ray-kurzweil-nanobots-brain-godlike_us_560555a0e4b0af3706dbe1e2 (accessed 28th June 2017)

11.

techno-mutation

- merging into a new psychosphere

11. techno-mutation – merging into a new psychosphere

mjuːˈteɪʃ(ə)n/

noun

the action or process of mutating.
the changing of the structure of a gene, resulting in a variant form which may be transmitted to subsequent generations.

'We are now dealing with the two major forces of social consciousness and techno-evolution, and their merging.'

Franco 'Bifo' Berardi, *Futurability*

The relations between technology and life are being reprogramed. We are yet to come out the other side; and when we do it may be likely that we will not recognize ourselves. The mutation underway may be that significant.

It took millennia to shift from the oral traditions into the alphabetical forms, handwritten onto papyruses and scrolls by dedicated scribes. Then we developed the mechanical arts of communication, from the printing press to telegraph, and then to the cabled telephone. Now, we have taken relatively little evolutionary time to jump into the digital infosphere that combines sensory (visual and tactile) with cognitive (brain patterns) in new modes of interaction. This new form of participation – or psychosphere – will have transformative implications for our social behavior and psychological patterning. Already the fabric of the world itself has undergone mutation as information spreads into our physical environment and into our devices. The very fabric of human experience is set to undergo a radical transformation as we begin to lose grip upon the rigidity of our biological form. We are moving away from a domain that has shaped the understanding of the human condition since *cogito ergo sum* and before.

We have lived until now with the largely dominant paradigm of 'us' within the human body and the rest of the world (everything else) 'out there.' We moved through our environments as if wrapped in a resistant cocoon, membrane-protected, as we collected our experiences of the world. Yet now this solidity is dissolving as we become increasingly porous to the digital-informational flows that are penetrating through our lives. The vibrant world of the digital-electronic has awoken – or been awakened – and is inserting itself (or being inserted?) into our organic reality-band. We may find ourselves compelled to evolve/adapt to a new frequency range as the organic-electronic (the biological-digital) forges a new universe of meaning for us. It will also be a new universe of communication where consciousness, digital-information, and augmented environments develop into a mutually participating exchange of symbols, signs, and significance. The social is now merging with the infosphere to form a new mutation. The result of this is that as we emerge from these bardo years we will need to reconstitute what the 'social' means. The earlier notions of a communal social body, with recognizable cognitive and geographical form, has now fragmented into a myriad of diverse rhythms as global human cultures mesh into an updated temporal-spatial mix. The present will no longer be linear. The future from here is not a straight line.

We have been hanging onto our linear models of living for so long we seem unable to think beyond the rigidity of mono-categories. We were the hunter-gatherers, then we had the agricultural revolution, and this finally became the industrial revolution. Now we are nearly sixty percent urban as a global species. We are classified by whether we are agricultural or urban dwellers when in fact we are temporal-spatial dwellers with ever-increasing access to new digital realms. For those people with access (and this is still a contested issue) – and who desire for access – there are possibilities for almost daily upgrades on cognitive experiences. We have begun to shift into an era whereby the 'cognitive dweller' will eradicate older geographical categories and definitions. As a species we are coalescing an architecture of overarching connectivity that is meshing fleshy bodies and material infrastructures with thinking patterns, ideas and immaterial forms, with automated algorithms. The planet that we once knew – and have treated with abominable cruelty - is morphing into a bio-info super-organism. Yet from where shall we derive our meaning in this? If the super-organism of which we form a part plugs into an 'unreal digital-material machine' then we may soon find ourselves belonging more to the programmed and automated codes of algorithmic conduct.

This mutation of our environment into technological-complexes is occurring at a pace more rapid than any mutation in known human experience. It is changing faster than our cultural habits and social conditionings and is stressing our thinking patterns to the max. We are forced to drop older mental models within one generation if we wish to navigate the current condition. Philosopher Franco Berardi believes that

> 'The acceleration of the infosphere produces an impoverishment of experience, because we are exposed to a growing mass of stimuli that we cannot elaborate intensively, or deeply know and perceive. More information, less meaning. More stimuli, less pleasure.'[1]

Allen Ginsberg's famous beat poem 'Howl' spoke of the 'angelheaded hipsters burning for the ancient heavenly connection to the starry dynamo in the machinery of night' as they burned within for some kind of sacred communion. As a human being we crave for connection, experience, and meaning. A techno-mutation is underway in these bardo times, and we must ask ourselves where this is taking us.

In the Machinery of Night

We have now reached a point whereby we need to de-activate the old programming that conditioned our thinking patterns and to establish new mental modes and conceptions. We have metamorphized from our caterpillar-like cocoons that held us in the larvae stage of human evolution as creatures separated from their environment. We are being pushed out into a huge expanse of meta-connectivity. With this forced push we are obliged to renegotiate our relations of being and meaning and to re-synchronize with a new form of world coming into being. The hyperreality that we are mutating into is a multiplicity of flows that is likely to develop into an unprecedented species social mind. The pre-digital world was reduced to crude measurement and then to social techniques of management that was called 'modernity.' The need for rationality led to a measurement of everything – even the unseen energies beyond the atom. Now the bardo times are propelling us into transformations that will reach far into the long-term horizon and beyond our historical grasp. We are now dealing with potentials and possibilities far outside our established perceptions and frames of reference. Until now we have lived largely within the perceivable; now it is a non-visible, unperceived range that demands our attention. We need to develop a light for the new machinery of night we have wandered into.

Even the notions of a 'modern age' are in disarray as less-developed regions leapfrog into high-technology and high-developed regions betray a less-than-civilized conduct. Within this uncertainty of what age, era, zone we are in – which is why this is referred to as the liminal 'bardo times' – we also share an unknowability about how our artificially smart machinic flows and digital dependencies will treat us. And yet we are too far embedded into the process now to even think of turning back, as we are propelled into an accelerating slipstream of transition. The only thing we can do now is to learn how to adapt to it – and to learn more about ourselves in the process. As we delve deeper into our technologized environments we will experience new contexts and thus new responses. We can either be empowered from this or cut off from it. We will be faced with a choice of embrace or evasion; of accepting this new environment or of resisting it – similar to how an organ transplanted into its new host body can respond. Resistance will leave us without a social body, and thus the organ withers.

There is no doubt that a techno-mutation has arisen, and it is affecting our perceptual senses. This mutation must be recognized and examined in order for us to understand the experience of the world we are moving into. In effect we have, as Franco Berardi terms it, entered into a *technomaya* where we are forced to undergo a changed set of experiential relations with the world: 'We live in the multilayered dimension of technomaya. Digital technology has given the media the power to act directly upon the mind, so that the mediasphere casts a spell that envelops the psychosphere.'[2] We cannot resist the mutation; to do so, according to Berardi, would be a technophobic act. We need to confront the fact that our experiences of the world are going to be increasingly mutated by technology as a new model of the psychosphere emerges. Humanity, as a collective cognitive organism, will develop a new set of responses to information stimuli. Our use of language, symbols, visuals, imagination – the way we use our memory – will undergo a change.

Berardi believes that this shows we have transitioned from the sphere of historical humanism to that of evolutionary automatism. Also, that the cognitive mutation induced by digital technology can be described as building a kind of techno-totalitarianism. Are these the new mutations of power?

Mutations of power

Our human past is littered with social revolutions of one kind or another. Whereas previously an accumulation of disruption was likely to lead into a revolution; today, it leads instead into the further consolidation of power. And in highly complex societies power becomes unknown, then intangible, and finally immaterial. The extreme of this is likely to be an automated form of incorporeal power wielded by the non-visible and the untouchable. As already discussed, power and authority today are pervasive throughout our societies to the point that they are impermeable to tangible resistance. To struggle will be like making mime. No official declaration of war has been made, yet the site of human consciousness is an open battlefield, and each mind counts as a combat zone.

The emergence of a connective (collective?) psychosphere lends itself to a new form of power relations that combine traceability with predictability, determinism, and control. The cloud where we upload our files and make our connections can be the same space that clouds our independent thought and action. And with the rise of techno-customization on the part of the major tech-monopolies we are increasingly moving around within the 'filter bubbles' of our own creation. Our traced behavior further customizes our actions into recorded predictability. The very act of techno-customization reduces our behavior into probability and predictability. Once this happens then pre-emption becomes a standardized tool within the repertoire of power relations. Berardi sees this as becoming a form of techno-totalitarianism in the making –

> '...as a process of standardization of cognition, perception, and behaviour based on the inscription of techno-linguistic automatisms in human communication, and therefore in the connective mind. This form of techno-totalitarianism results from three consecutive steps.'[3]

Berardi then goes on to describe these three steps as comprising i) the permanent connective wiring of interactions between humans; ii) the replacement of living experience; and iii) the insertion of techno-devices and enhancement of neural programming.

The first step - the permanent connective wiring of interactions between humans – Berardi refers to as a process of *cellularization*. This process he describes as the 'perfect carrier' of the socio-cognitive mutation. The mobile/cellular phone, in particular, has created an infrastructure of global interconnection and opens the way to what Berardi sees as the 'ultimate deterritorialization' and ubiquity of information. He sees it as leading to the 'collectivization of personal lives' whereby individualism is subsumed into a form of commercial singularity. *Cellularization* also sets up a techno-linguistic system of exchange whereby people become less independent actors of their own behavior and more controlled by the new techno-linguistic parameters. Social communication thus becomes subsumed into the 'electronic swarm,' as Berardi puts it. Language becomes more a form spoken by the technological system rather than technology being a subject of language.

The second step - the replacement of living experience – is similar to what has been discussed throughout this book regarding hyperreality and the notion of simulation. It regards the replacement of current lived experience with the simulations of standardized and automated stimulus. We can also see this creeping form of replacement occur through the advancement of automations, augmented-reality, and the 'phantom performance' (see Chapter 7). There is a gradual acceptance of the 'replacement' of the lived experience. Experience is more than an event, it is a sensual encounter and the independent responses taken away from those encounters. If this process is somehow standardized, or customized-controlled, then we can see how Berardi views this as an act of techno-totalitarianism.

The third step - the insertion of techno-devices and enhancement of neural programming – moves away from the cognitive-psychological focus of the previous two steps and enters into the terrain of hardware. It refers to the manipulation of neural systems through devices, prostheses, modifiers, and enhancers. Neural manipulation through biological, chemical, or technological intervention will be a huge area for exploration and experimentation in the future, if it isn't already now. It also suggests acting upon our known neuroplasticity to create and reshape neuro-synaptic pathways. It opens the way for pharma-corporations – as well as authoritarian bodies – to enact psycho-sabotage or subversion through neuro-dominance. It is a dangerous terrain indeed, and the genii is already out of the box on this one.

Berardi asks whether it is possible, or even advisable, to resist the current mutation. He concludes that resistance may not be possible because technological innovation invariably reshapes the social environment. To resist would be to place the person first on the margins of their social milieu, and eventually outside forever (if this were permissible). A person, and their family lineage, would effectively cease to exist. The matrix of techno-totalitarianism would erase their data completely or absorb them utterly.

Also, as neuroplasticity adapts our brains to the newly emerging social environments, we would be faced with the decision to adapt or disentangle from our known world. As the infosphere of our social environments becomes increasingly filled with propaganda, fake news, manipulated audio, video, and visual images, we will find ourselves dominated as well as drawn into an upsurge of cognitive mutation. Our psychosphere will become a whole new territory for us, and for those to come.

The State of the Psychosphere

Our environments are now taking on a different rhythm; different landscapes will bring new sensory experiences and contexts for our neural states. How will we react? The accelerating development of autonomous technology and algorithmic systems will bring unprecedented change into our lives. For some, especially those who still belong to an earlier pre-bardo epoch, it will bring disruptions into lives and into social relations. As conscious organisms we must be prepared for both disruption and mutation – they come hand in hand. The entire nervous system of the human species will undergo a transformation – a re-wiring? – as the techno-mutation itself shifts from a novelty into a normality. As a species we are set to undergo an evolutionary transmutation that will encompass the biological-cognitive-social-technological systems that frame our known reality. Some people may refer to this as transhumanism, yet the entire history of life on this planet has been about mutation in all its forms. Yet now this process is speeding up as it is being both naturally and deliberately manufactured and enhanced. Its impacts will apply to each one of us as we are faced with a new

> 'The process of transformation, which was the object of political imagination in modernity, is shifting to the conceptual and practical sphere of neuroplasticity. The mutation of the mind is underway. It is the consequence of a spasmodic attempt by individual minds to cope with a chaotic global infosphere, and to reframe the relation between the psychosphere and the infosphere, between cognition and stress, and between the brain and chaos.'[4]

The world we are in now offers to us a modified psychological dimension. In the beginning some of us may experience trauma or senses overload. A new adaptation to re-shaped environmental conditions can involve some suffering, which may induce new and extreme forms of mental madness.

How can we be redeemed from this? Is there the possibility – the hope – of psycho-salvation? Could it be that within the mutation-machine there are viruses/ memes that are both bad and good? Perhaps within all this reshuffle that is the bardo times – the hyperreality, the hoax, the simulations, the high-velocity, the illusory nature of reality, the techno-mutations – there is always the possibility for the rediscovery, recovery, and redemption of the human soul. After all, is not everything only an illusion – a maya or *techno-maya* – in order to drive us further toward knowing our very Source?

Perhaps the Source-Code has been programmed within our reality all along and we only failed to see its flickering lights. Maybe there is a code, a set of signs and symbols, that are scattered throughout the social-technical matrix that is our modern lives. The bardo times may be a trigger compelling us into re-cognition. The virus may be a mutation that can free us as much as it subsumes us. Could the choice be ours?

Perhaps we ourselves are the incandescent flickers of redemptive hope within the unreal gnostic-machine of our reality-matrix.

A Bardo Chat with: Janus, Roman God of beginnings, transitions, passages, and endings.

Author (A): Hello, is that Janus?

Janus (J): Greetings. This is Janus.

A: Greetings to you, Janus. Your arrival is very welcome, and fitting to what I wanted to talk about.

J: Yes. My timing is always appropriate. That is why I am the god and patron of beginnings, transitions, and endings. And what kind of a god of beginnings and endings would I be if I had no sense of correct timing? You would not wish for a beginning to be delayed or an ending to come too soon, would you?

A: Quite so. And it is fitting because it was beginnings and endings that I wished to talk about.

J: Naturally, that is why I am here and you are here. You humans may think everything in your life is a random coincidence, but from our perspective it is not. I suggest you try the bigger perspective some time. It would greatly benefit you.

A: Thank you. Yes, I have been striving for a sense of the bigger picture most of my life. It's not easy when you're a human. We tend to live our whole lives with what's just in front of our eyes. My grandparents never lived anywhere else except the town where they were born. And we all grow up with the ideas planted in us by our parents and community. Our lives were often sheltered. There was no sense of the 'bigger picture.' Now the world is different. Everyone being born into the world today is naturally hard-wired for a bigger-picture perspective.

J: That is correct. Many of you humans had a larger perspective in your history. That is, in your earlier years. Yet this larger perspective was often aligned with either a mythological or a religious-mystical view. You always relied upon a delivery method, something to bring these larger views to you. That is also one of the reasons why we came to you in the guise of gods. You were unable to receive information unless it corresponded to specific parameters of thinking. And for a long time in your human history these parameters were what you would call 'quasi-religious.' You were unable to see alone, through your own senses. Your intelligence was attached to certain cultural forms. That is why everything, even today, must be delivered to you in an appropriate way.

A: And what would happen if this information arrived to us in ways that were not 'appropriate'?

J: As has always been the case. The information is either rejected or the carrier – the way of transmission – is attacked. That is why those of us whom you call 'gods' also have to appear to you in ways that you can assimilate within certain of your psychological patterns. And this is how we are communicating right now. You have this mental framework of a god called Janus, who represents a range of functions. And this is who I am to you.

A: And who are you to others, or to yourself?

J: This is neither relevant nor useful to you right now. So, back to your initial question - tell me what it is about beginnings and endings that you wished to know of.

A: Well, I understand that phases in human history have their cycles – their beginnings and endings – and that at certain times, in particular epochs, we pass through a transition period that is especially momentous. Isn't that so?

J: Yes, that is so; according to how your reality operates through matter. The cycles that operate within your realm have, more or less, always been in this way. These patterns have always been there for your historians to see. They are like programs that are self-regulating and can be left to continue on their own. These unfoldings, or transitions, also mark the passages of time on your planet. That is, these beginnings and endings are time-markers for your reality. They provide the sense of linear sequence. Or what you call progress and development. Other domains have their own passages and transitions too; although beginnings and endings are something that is specific to your dimensional realm.

A: And why is that?

J: It is because your reality is perceived as being linear. This is largely an earth-bound perspective. And at the two, and even three, dimensional level this perspective is largely correct. However, it is inaccurate and a very limited understanding. Yet it works for where you are at now. Without going into detail, I can say that outside of your constrictive reality there is no sense of beginning and end – everything is connected and conceptual, not linear. By perceiving sequence, you are able to see things in specific positions. Because you have yet to develop a consciousness of correspondence where everything is related, you are given to perceive things in positions. To put it another way, in your modern terminology, you see the islands but not the underlying water that connects them. In your terms, you understand a movement from one place to another. In this way, one door closes and another opens.

A: Yes, I think I get that. And that is also what I wanted to ask. My sense is that right now, using this terminology, we are closing one door upon our history and are opening another. I mean, we are opening a doorway into a new epoch and so we are in that transition from stepping out of one doorway and entering into another. Is that so?

J: Yes, it is. Of course, this is only true from the perspective that pertains to your reality. And you have made these crossings many times before in your long history. Some of them were made before what you call your 'history' even began. But now I speak only of your current phase in human civilization. It is an important transition that you are currently in.

A: Yes, I feel this. And I'm sure I am not alone here. There are many people who feel similar about our present epoch. Can you tell me why this is so?

J: I can explain a little; only so much as to not affect the agency of free will amongst your species.

A: Okay, thanks. Please go ahead.

J: There is a convergence of many areas of change, and they have all come together at the same time. Some of them concern your social systems and historic forces, as is normal. Yet there are other changes occurring within the human being itself that will provide an extra ingredient. I can tell you that you are also changing from within, from the very fiber of your bodies. All this will affect your human consciousness. And thirdly, there is change occurring within your planet as she adjusts to prepare for her new position in space and energy. All these factors together are resulting in what your historians will look back on and call a 'historic period' of change. This moment in your history will never be forgotten, just as you have not forgotten the Scientific Revolution or the end of your mediaeval period. You have been in a modern dark age, despite your industrial growth and technologies. Within the human soul, within your minds and your hearts, you have still been as if in the dark ages. Now all that is set to change. Have you understood?

A: Yes. Well, I understand what you say; although I'm not sure if I fully understand the workings of it.

J: That is correct, and to be expected. There will be few humans who will understand the true nature of this transition upon your planet. There are reasons for this, but they do not concern you.

A: Yes, okay. Could you say something more about us being in the modern dark ages?

J: Yes. You often confuse consciousness with matter. Your paradigms of growth, development and progress are all matter-based. That is, they are materialistic paradigms. They do not correlate to true awareness, knowledge, or understanding. How you manipulate matter, which are your objects, is not a question of true progress. Your Dark Ages brought you out of mythology and into matter, so to speak. Then your industrial ages gave you the means and tools to develop your relationship with things of matter. Yet you have ignored that which truly matters - and this is consciousness. Matter comes from consciousness and not the other way around. You continue to obsess yourself with secondary phenomenon. This is a sign that you are still, as a species, in the dark ages. You have yet to awaken to the true power and presence of consciousness. Until you do so you will remain within the dark, regardless of the trickery of your machines.

A: And so, this transition that you speak of is about moving us out of the dark and into an awareness of consciousness?

J: Yes, that is so. the transition that stands before you, so to speak, is a monumental one in your history as a species. It is about a recognition - an understanding - of the fundamental underlying energies of your realm. And this is a question of consciousness. This is primary. All other elements, no matter how sophisticated they are, belong to the secondary.

A: And so, this future towards a recognition of the fundamental reality of consciousness awaits us?

J: Yes, it does. Although I cannot give you any frames of reference in terms of time. This is flexible, and changes constantly. But rest assured that you are moving through portals, and the future that awaits you is beyond your present perceptions. I can tell you though that it will be beyond your imaginings. There is so much that awaits you – from one door and through another.

A: Yes, thank you. This corresponds with my own intuition. Yet right now we are experiencing turbulent times.

J: Changing tides always create turbulence in their wake. This is the pattern of all material things, as well as energetic states – both here and beyond your realm.

A: And I suppose that we shall get through this?

J: I suppose too. It is in your hands though; it always was and always shall be. You, or rather your species, are responsible for stepping through the doors. Beginnings and endings exist, yet where they take you is largely your doing.

A: Yes, that is true. And would you say that as part of the bigger picture what we are experiencing now is the turbulence of crossing this current transition?

J: As part of the bigger picture, yes. It is but a brief moment within the overall movement of development upon your planet. Yet for you it shall be a lifetime, or more.

A: (sigh) Yes, I suspected it would be. I might not live it out, yet this is beyond just one person.

J: You and your generation will live a great deal out and will witness some great changes. Stick around, there is more to come. As some of you humans often like to say - enjoy the ride!

A: Yeah, thanks for that - I certainly will, through the rough and the smooth.

J: Indeed, it shall be both of those. Yet where you are heading is beyond words. Head up, keep looking forward, and sacred speed to you. The rest is up to you - to all of you. You are greater than you know. Do not downplay your ability. Deep faith and courage - and look both ways! (low laugh).

A: Thank you, Janus. I will; I mean we all will - keep moving ahead, with courage. Thank you for those final words.

J: Always remember yourself. Now I say goodbye.

A: Goodbye, Janus.

Endnotes

[1] Berardi, Franco. 2015. *AND: Phenomenology of the End*. South Pasadena, CA: Semiotext(e), p187

[2] Berardi, Franco. 2015. *AND: Phenomenology of the End*. South Pasadena, CA: Semiotext(e), p299

[3] Berardi, Franco. 2015. *AND: Phenomenology of the End*. South Pasadena, CA: Semiotext(e), p311

[4] Berardi, Franco. 2015. *AND: Phenomenology of the End*. South Pasadena, CA: Semiotext(e), p318

12.

the incandescent flame

- gnostic flickers of redemption

12. the incandescent flame – gnostic flickers of redemption

ɪnkanˈdɛs(ə)nt/
adjective

emitting light as a result of being heated.
full of strong emotion; passionate.

'Life is a dream for the wise, a game for the fool, a comedy for the rich, a tragedy for the poor.'

Sholom Aleichem.

'In case I don't see ya, good afternoon, good evening and goodnight.'

Truman Burbank (from 'The Truman Show)

We've always lived with the same age-old dilemma of trying to decipher between appearance and reality. This impasse has often been like a conspirators' game played by different sides. From the Gnostic perspective it has been recognized as a grand cosmic conspiracy. And this conspiracy, like a mutation, has infiltrated our societies and cultures for generation after generation. Clues, signs, and indications, as well as possible tools, have been channelled through our cultures in various forms, awaiting the gaze of the watchful. And there have always been those who saw the anomalies, and who were marginalized and lived on the periphery of the dominant, ruling ideology. Many sages who saw the flickers within the program were outcast for fear their visions might incite a trickle of awareness to seep into consensus reality. It is the same today - from esteemed philosophers, renowned scientists, and millionaire technologists, to the general person in the street – we are beginning to question whether or not our reality is quite what it seems. Perhaps we are living in some sort of simulation after all, and everything is an elaborate game we must play out. This is what this entire book has been about.

In the 4th century BC the Chinese sceptical thinker Zhuang Zhou famously dreamed that he was a butterfly, and when he woke up he could not help wondering whether it had been Zhou dreaming that he was a butterfly, or whether it was now a butterfly dreaming that it was Zhou. Both 'realities' could be equally real. And so perhaps one of the ways out of this dilemma is to seek for the source code, the signs of our programmed reality. In recent years there have been debates running back and forth from scientists and philosophers about the discoveries that our universe is so finely tuned that it could not be the result of accident. There appears to be so many staggeringly coherent fine-tuning that not even the known age of our universe can account for it.[1] Discovering that we live in such a fine-tuned reality might be just one way of showing us that there is indeed a source code behind everything. And it seems that some influential people are taking this proposition seriously. A recent article in *The New Yorker* on life in Silicon Valley told of many people in the entrepreneurial tech-valley were now obsessed with the simulation hypothesis. It also mentioned that two tech billionaires had secretly engaged scientists to work on breaking us out of the simulation.[2] Elon Musk, the founder of SpaceX and Tesla Motors, is not the only one amongst us who thinks that there is only one possibility among billions that we are living in the 'base reality.' Maybe these techies are seeing some of the source code leaking through.

---

1 For more on this see my previous book The Sacred Revival: Magic, Mind, and Meaning in a Technological Age.

2 For more on this story, see - http://www.newyorker.com/magazine/2016/10/10/sam-altmans-manifest-destiny

There's no denying that there have been teachings operating throughout our cultures that have sought to attain glimpses of this illusive source code. We've had Hermeticism, Neo-Platonism, Gnosticism, alchemy, Cabbalah, magic/occult, as well as many other channels, unknown or unsuspected, that have attempted to infiltrate our sleeping minds. Our most prominent cultural distractions may sometimes also be carriers of the code, like the Trojan Horse that carried the Greek soldiers hidden within its hollow underbelly. Similarly, within the hollow underbelly of our mass entertainment may also lie some of the clues to the subterfuge of our living within this bardo realm. Cinema, while being a technology designed to substitute simulation for reality, may also hide the seeds of triggering awareness. It is, after all, an art form that is ideally suited to the notions of seduction and visual trickery. In some ways, cinema plays the ideal part of being a ruse for channelling the gnosis.

The Gnostic Underbelly

Such 'Gnostic cinema,' as it can be called, is rife with illusions pretending to be real when it is obvious they are not. We are given plentiful stereotypes pretending to be rebels; struggles for freedom against fate; the falsity of appearances; multiple ambiguities; the façade of the status quo; and the possibilities for transformation and its obstacles. Such cinema aims to show the viewer that within our social conformity there is an underlying sense and realization that 'something isn't quite right.' Films like *The Matrix Trilogy* and *The Truman Show* enact this paradox between outer conformity/struggle and inner realization. The extra paradox thrown in here is that such films also aim to be seductive and illusionary in order to attract the viewer. As in life there is a conflict between external packaging (image) and internal vision (reality). The movie industry is stuck within its own cage of trying to depict the illusion of reality and the possibility for transcendence, within its own strictures of material confinement and profit-making.

Films such as *The Matrix Trilogy* are aware that cinema is a deceptive form which the directors use to suggest that all material forms are illusory. Yet within a materially-based reality there is no other way. We are forced to make use of the materials at hand, and to let the light get in through the cracks. There is room for forms of legitimate imitation, which can protect the secret sigils and codes within. These are the jokers in the pack – the jester at the court of King Lear. Our cultural commodities

– our tales, stories, myths, and entertainment – are also the means of transmission. And in the bardo years it is even more crucial that some of us can see these flickers of illumination within the dark depths of the cultural cave. Perhaps this is what can be called a form of transcendental irony - working with the secret codes of evolutionary mutation through the material form of popular culture.

Cultural stories and narratives are ideal channels for the transmission of transcendental stimuli, such as hermetic wisdom, perennial truths, and Gnostic vision. In the past twenty-five years there has been an array of overtly Gnostic films, including *Total Recall* (1990 – remade 2012); *Pleasantville* (1998); *Dark City* (1998); *The Truman Show* (1998); *eXistenZ* (1999); *The Thirteenth Floor* (1999); *The Matrix* (1999), *Donnie Darko* (2001); *Vanilla Sky* (2001), *Cloud Atlas* (2012); *Prometheus* (2012); *Doctor Strange* (2016); and *Ghost in the Shell* (2017) – to name but a few. And then there is almost everything from Philip K. Dick.

Those films with a Gnostic theme often show ambiguous relationships that are between humans and machines; reality and dream fantasy; the interior psyche and material reality; evil and the angelic impulse. And through these dualistic struggles there is the underlying sense that despite the commercial core of Hollywood there is also something else - something almost otherworldly and unknowable - lurking within. The illusion of celluloid appearances transmits to us a vague feeling that something isn't quite right and makes us question our own sense of reality. We may pay the money and contribute to the business of commercial entertainment, yet the channel offers us more than one wavelength – if we are listening. We can be triggered through certain codes within our cultural artefacts, or we can be drawn further into their labyrinths. As Morpheus famously says to Neo at the beginning of *The Matrix* – 'You take the blue pill—the story ends, you wake up in your bed and believe whatever you want to believe. You take the red pill—you stay in Wonderland, and I show you how deep the rabbit hole goes.' As always in life, we get to choose to know more, or not; to wake up in our beds believing whatever we wish or exploring to see how deep the rabbit hole goes. It has been an age-old choice, which surprisingly few have taken. According to the Gnostic philosopher Basilides, the inhabitants of our planet are exiled at three hundred and sixty-five removes from reality. That's quite a deep rabbit hole, and surely not for the claustrophobic.

The good news is that we are never left without a

lifeline. Even in the densest of hyperrealities – in the smartest simulation and the deepest illusion - there are always signs and signposts dotted around. It is as if the Gnostic game designer has left clues coded throughout the game for those players aware enough to pick-up on them. The Gnostic vision not only unravels the falsity of the exoteric world but also points towards the potential path of transcendence. We can be reminded that,

> The images we took for reality float like ghosts. The words we held to be vessels of the real become veils. We think we're going mad. Most of us quickly seek help for our ostensible insanity and are eventually reprogrammed to dwell again in the dungeons of matter. A few of us, however, are forever altered, and we spend our lives wondering how to shed the images and words that block the light. We become silent and ignorant.[1]

In this silence we enter into a new and more refined state of constant watchfulness. It is a state where we attempt to negate the distracting noise of the world; and we are ignorant too because knowledge, in a world of illusions, can only be illusory. Like puppets with our strings pulled we have been guilty of mistaking ignorance for knowledge. At the same time each one of us is a whisker away from that internal glance which lights a spark of intuition that leads upon the road of Gnostic understanding. As if coming out of a dark machinic night some of us are slowly awakening from a catatonic state. Welcome to the show.

Welcome to the Show

One of the most entertaining and accurate portrayals of the Gnostic vision in cinema in recent years is *The Truman Show* (1998). Directed by Peter Weir and written by Andrew Niccol, this popular film is well-known to many of us, and tells the story of the character Truman Burbank (played by Jim Carrey) whose life is a live reality show, unbeknown to him. The television producer named Christof (played by Ed Harris) is the Gnostic demiurge (creator god) who has created an artificial world - a huge domed town with computer-controlled weather patterns, fake sky and sea, and populated by actors playing their scripted parts. He has created a simulated world, a simulacrum of the real, where everything *seems* to be true but is not. We know this because we are the 'viewers' outside, looking in (we are in fact the viewers of the viewers of the drama). The principle character of Truman Burbank is ignorant of his condition and of the nature of his world. To him everything is real, which is not surprising as we would no doubt think the same if we were in his place. His life has been created (manipulated) to exist as a character in his own television show. He is watched 24/7, fed false information, and his dreams are constantly dashed or talked down by those around him. He lives in an unseen prison from which he is unable to escape for he does not consider escape a necessity. The character of Truman is both a prisoner of his false reality as well as a prisoner to a consumerist culture industry. And yet, as is central to the Gnostic vision, something eventually triggers Truman - he falls in love.

Truman (true man) notices the beautiful Sylvia (played by Natascha McElhone) who from afar attracts him with her presence. Because she is just a vision to him, someone he has yet to meet, she exists outside of his everyday mundane, tangible material existence. He sees, recognizes, something in her that provides him with a vision, and this ultimately becomes his liberating catalyst. After she is taken away from him (to leave the show forever) for breaking the 'game rules,' Truman is motivated to leave his old world - to seek his beloved (the archetypal Gnostic quest). Yet this longing within him creates a feeling of melancholy (detachment from Source). It is through this melancholy that Truman begins to notice things he hadn't recognized before - the same people saying the same things at precisely the same time, and odd anomalies appearing in his 'reality.' In other words, he has been triggered into awareness, and now he is able to see his world from a different perspective. His eventual planned escape culminates in an almost mythical voyage across the sea. Despite his conditioned fear of water, he plunges himself into the abyss. He shows that he is ready to die, to sacrifice himself, in order to secure his liberation. In mystical terminology, he is ready to 'die before you die' in order to shed his old life. Finally, he reaches the 'end' of his world and arrives at the door (portal) to what is for him another reality. Yet before he leaves his old world the voice of Christof - his 'creator god' (demiurge) - addresses him in a soft voice. He tells Truman that he is safer within this world; that he is protected and loved. 'Was nothing real?' asks Truman. Christof replies that he, Truman, was real. And that since there are lies and deceit on both sides, there is no difference, and thus he would be better to choose the sanctuary of security over the unknown. Truman, now knowing the false reality in which he lives, decides that the truth is a price worth paying for. He takes a bow and leaves the stage.

The camera then shifts to scenes of millions of people all over the world watching blank, static screens as the real-time live feed is cut. Their ongoing addictive dose of reality TV has been cut off. The last viewers we are shown are two parking garage attendants whom seem stunned at first. Then they reach for another piece of pizza and turn over the channel to see what else might be on television to watch. As the film finishes, what do *we* do? We leave the cinema or turn off the television and go and do something else. We have been the real viewers all along, and this is the Gnostic twist. Everything is just television, an enjoyable piece of entertainment. It's not real. And then we go about our business, as we have always done, as if our own scripts have been written. As film critic Eric Wilson notes,

> Public and private are not distinct. We are all playing roles, all enacting the lifestyles on the television; we are all being watched by others, commodified and consumed...There is no difference between each one of us and Truman. If Truman and his world are controlled, then we are all controlled.[2]

Yet we may also question ourselves, as we walk away from the film - have we somehow been triggered? Did we recognize something within *The Truman Show* that reflects our own existence?

This film could be said to have parallels with the ancient Gnostic tale of 'The Precious Jewel' -

> *In a remote realm of perfection, there was a just monarch who had a wife and a wonderful son and daughter. They all lived together in happiness.*
>
> *One day the father called his children before him and said: 'The time has come, as it does for all. You are to go down, an infinite distance, to another land. You shall seek and find and bring back a precious Jewel.'*
>
> *The travellers were conducted in disguise to a strange land, whose inhabitants almost all lived a dark existence. Such was the effect of this place that the two lost touch with each other, wandering as if asleep. From time to time they saw phantoms, similitudes of their country and of the Jewel, but such was their condition that these things only increased the depth of their reveries, which they now began to take as reality.*
>
> *When news of his children's plight reached the king, he sent word by a trusted servant, a wise man: 'Remember your mission, awaken from your dream, and remain together.'*
>
> *With this message they roused themselves, and with the help of their rescuing guide they dared the monstrous perils which surrounded the Jewel, and by its magic aid returned to their realm of light, there to remain in increased happiness for evermore.*[3]

We live amidst the Gnostic flickers of redemption. As slumbering souls within the hoax of our material illusion we seek those signs and codes that were left for us in artefacts, old and new, that may trigger us into awareness once again. Indeed, we feel reassured that there exists the possibility, the potential, to be awakened. Yet once triggered into awareness we are then confronted with a similar dilemma that faced Truman. Do we continue in our old lives knowing that it is all a grand illusion, a fake, a simulation? Or do we take the plunge into the abyss and be willing to 'die before you die' in order to find the truth? Do we have the urge, the drive, which motivated Truman to finally reject the comfort and security offered to him by his 'creator'? Could we make that decision to walk through the door and to throw away all that we have known in our lives? Truman – the 'true man' – did, and he reached his goal.

Has anything clicked yet? The bardo times can be dark, filled with apprehension and uncertainty, yet we must move toward the light, before our wings are clipped forever. The flickers of the internal flame are never subdued totally for they linger on within our deepest depths. They yearn toward recognition, toward a spark from the awakening mind. But what if our minds are sleeping too deeply?

Meister Eckhart said 'If you haven't the truth of

which we are speaking in yourselves, you cannot understand me.' This is the heart of the Gnostic way, and which tells us that the first move must come from within each of us. We are compelled to find that dim flicker within us first. We may not always find our goal by seeking, and yet seeking is the first condition required of us. The psychologist Maurice Nicoll commented that the highest possible level of each person is said to be within us, and yet many people consider that it refers to a state attainable after death, in some future time. Few are those that realize that there exists a possibility now for this transcendence toward a level of perception beyond our current state. And yet it is through the here and now of the material world we are forced to work.

Flickers of Light

Many mystics have told that the preliminary knowledge can be gained by ordinary means, from existing and known sources that are accessible to all. Did you really think the bardo realm would leave you all alone, without an Ariadne's thread? Yet the Gnostic path does not attempt to missionize or to convince people of its presence or its truth. It does not need to. It is down to each person who must convince themselves whether they are sincere and genuine in their seeking. Everything comes back to *us* – we are part of the coding. The flickers of light that fleetingly adorn our reality, and our bardo realm, are but the embers of a greater truth that we have all been blinded to. This knowledge cannot be gained or understood unless we first make some corresponding room for it within us. We are both the walker and the path. And one of the first steps to be taken is to recognize, and accept, that our idea and view of the world is only a description of the simulation that beguiles us. As the mystic Iskandar of Balkh once proclaimed – 'You shall become aware, through daily practice, that what you imagine to be your self is concocted from beliefs put into you by others, and is not your self at all.' And still the flickers of light illuminate the darkness. Yet why the darkness?

It is dark because the veil cast over us seeks our continued distraction with the mechanical delights of the lower world. It does not wish for us to see things *as they really are*. Instead we have the simplified stories that are told to us over and over again that finally make us believe in the hyperreality, in the great hoax. Our world, like Truman Burbank's, is a grand show directed by a megalomaniac producer who pulls the strings and orchestrates the set pieces. We are living in a costume period drama, like those so favored by British television and exported across the globe. Only by realizing that our heart is blind do we begin to gain the first slither of sight. Until we can feel this longing for the genuine flame within we continue to remain attracted, like the moth, to the larger flame offered by the simulations of entertainment, success, wealth, achievement, fame, and so on. And on and on it goes until we reach a final loneliness that only becomes a regret when we smell the hand of death approaching.

There are incredible times ahead of us, beckoning us into the future. Their treasured goods await us, untouched. They shall not be released until the human soul opens its heart and says 'Enough! – now show me the *Real*.' And this moment of asking is what the darkness fears most. Yet in the bardo times we can still ask, and still receive. The Source Code is listening out for our call, always and forever. We are being urged to find the *precious jewel* and to bring it home, before Disney makes a movie out of it.

In the end, all that we can truly do is to seek the freedom of the human soul. Incandescent angels, awake from the machinery of night!

A Bardo Chat with: Morpheus, Greek God of dreams.

Author (A): Hello, are you there?

Morpheus (M): I guess that depends on which 'you' you are referring to.

A: Sorry, but I always half expect someone else to turn up. Each time it's always a pleasant surprise.

M: (low chuckle) How human of you! Always a pleasant surprise you say. Well, I am Morpheus, and I hope you find me a pleasant surprise to your liking.

A: Hello Morpheus. It is a pleasure indeed. And thank you for turning up for this quick chat.

M: Not a problem, I was just passing – as you earthlings like to say. Besides, I can be here and many other places simultaneously so it's not a bother; unless you bore me, that is.

A: Well, I certainly hope I won't be boring you. And since you are the god of dreams you're just the person I wish to speak with.

M: And how's that? Tell me more. Are you going to request me to enter into someone's dreams to influence them? This is what I normally get asked for by humans. They pray and beg me to enter into the dreams of someone they know, which is usually their loved one (chuckle). Ah, humans are nothing if not predictable! So, tell me, do you have someone whom you'd like me to make fall in love with you?

A: Well, yes and no. But that's not the point, and it's not why I'm here. I wish to speak about our collective dreams, as a species.

M: Ah, you wish to enquire over the bigger picture, the bigger dream. Yes, that's the one you least suspect, and which influences your species the most. All of your civilizations have been born from this collective dream, in one way or another.

A: That's what I suspected. Perhaps you could say a little of how this works?

M: I could, yet there is only so much I can tell you. I'm not wishing to be rude, but your species has not yet arrived at the place where, by its own free will, it can receive and understand all that there is to know. Information comes according to your capacity to receive and understand it. If I tell you something that is beyond the remit of your capacity, it may in fact hinder you or confuse you.

A: Can you tell me something?

M: Yes, I can tell you something; and I shall, for it is permitted at this time. I say permitted because we have seen the potentials of your species on this planet at this time, and you have made a step towards your next phase of evolution. Soon much more information will be released to you; for now, I shall share a little.

A: Thanks.

M: There is a collective dream of the species, as you call it. Yet it does not belong solely to yourselves. It is shared by all, including other species on your planet as well as the planet itself. Although we can call it a collective dream, in truth this is not accurate. It is more like an information field. And all things on your planet are a part of this information field. And sentient creatures, such as yourselves, can both receive and transmit into this field. During your sleep state you are active within this field, receiving more than transmitting.

A: And this is where we get our dreams from - our ideas and our inspirations?

M: Correct. And through this field humanity is provided information and knowledge that guides you. You do not need to be sleeping in order to receive information from this field. It is continually communicating with you, beyond your awareness. By being alive you are participating within this field. It is a living intelligence. It doesn't dream as it is always awake. It is the human species who are dreaming, living their lives half awake. The more you awaken, the more you will receive and understand this living intelligence field.

A: And are we continually transmitting back into this field?

M: Correct. That is so. The minds of humanity are also feeding back into this field, for better or for worse.

A: Why do you say for worse?

M: I say that because your thought forms also influence the collective field, which in turn affects the energy of your planet. Disruptive, angry, chaotic thought forms add to the potential disharmony of the planet. What you dream indeed comes to fruition, in one way or another. And you do not need to be asleep for this to function. Each of your thoughts, your emotions, in every moment - they fold back into this living intelligence field. Individually this is not such an issue. It is when you collectively share a particular thought form - an emotion of trauma, let us say. If this is shared amongst many of you then there is a disturbance in the field. Dreams interact both ways.

A: And so, the Muses really do exist?

M: (low chuckle). Yes, they do. They form part of the potentials in this field of dreams, if you will. What inspires you comes from this communication.

A: And you say that we have taken a step forward in our evolution? Does this mean we are soon going to exit our current period of transition? I have often referred to these transition years as bringing temporary disruption.

M: You will exit these tumultuous years. However, when and how will be down to your own making. This is all a part of your collective free will. Yet the potentials are there. As you often like to say – it is only a matter of time.

A: And are we really waking up, as a species?

M: Yes, of course – and you were always meant to! Yet do not get too excited, it is not an overnight thing. You must think in terms of generations.

A: Sure, I suspected that. One last question: has the field been responsible for leaving signs and guidance within our cultures, for our awakening?

M: Yes and no. It is not as simple as that. There has been guidance and teachings, of course, from the very beginning. Many of these signs do originate from the living intelligence field of which I have spoken. Yet there are also those 'signs' – as you call them – that are placed within your cultures by those who live and operate within your cultures.

A: This is interesting. And who have these people – these 'operatives' – been? Can you tell me more?

M: I can tell you no more than you already know or suspect. Many of these 'operatives,' as you say, have been known to you throughout history. And many more have not. Those you know, you know; and those you don't, you don't. I can say no more than this. You have been capable of receiving this information. More will come as you proceed. So, don't forget to keep dreaming - as you humans like to say.

A: Indeed not. We can never forget to dream, but at the same time we must be awake, right?

M: That is so. A pleasant conundrum, you might say. May it please you, and may it take you forward. Keep awake in your dreams. And now I feel it is time to leave.

A: Thank you, Morpheus. It has been a pleasure. Goodbye!

M: So long, for now…

Endnotes

[1] Wilson, Eric G. 2006. *Secret Cinema: Gnostic Vision in Film*. London: Continuum, p37.

[2] Wilson, Eric G. 2006. *Secret Cinema: Gnostic Vision in Film*. London: Continuum, p46.

[3] Shah, I. 1971. *Thinkers of the East*. London: Jonathan Cape, p123.

Afterword

ɑːftəwəːd/

noun

a concluding section in a book.

'The world has no being except as an appearance;
From end to end its state is a sport and a play.'

Shabistari

There is more to life than just living in survival mode. It often seems, when we look at the world around us, that survival is perhaps the best we can do under present circumstances. As I have addressed throughout this book, we are in a tumultuous momentary phase as we pass from one particular era, or mode of life, to another. These years of transition, which I have named as 'bardo times,' are darker than what we would normally expect precisely because the old ways, the old systems, are struggling to maintain their supremacy. The status quo never likes to let go, as history has taught us repeatedly. Despite many things appearing to be on the negative side, what we are witnessing is rather the recalibration that is going on both within our societies and within ourselves. The two sides go together as threads woven within a delicate tapestry. We live as part of a larger mass culture where populations and cities are growing, and conflicts and problems exist globally that affect us locally too. There is no doubt that the psychological implications of this are major, and often overwhelm the individual. At times our problems seem beyond the scope of our ability to cope. As a collective species, and within our diverse cultures and societies, we live and express the human condition, with all its flaws and wonder.

The average person expects our disruptive upheavals and cultural changes to solve all problems, after which our societies will readjust and return to a fair degree of normalcy (whatever that may mean). Yet the fault in this perspective is viewing the source of all our ills as residing in the external, physical environment. In fact, the truth is the reverse; the source for real, lasting, permanent change has always – and always will – reside within the interior of the human being. And although we humans exist as social creatures as part of our communities (local and/or global), we also require a certain degree of personal individuation. Change and transformation radiates outwards as well as internally. The contrary to this is becoming a 'mass-minded' person who is submerged into the general mass movement of society, which fosters dependence, imitation, a lessening of personal vision and insight, and conditioning to a lower level of consciousness. It also creates a mass arena for the projection of our emotions, frustration, and negative thoughts; which in turn all coalesce to maintain, and sustain, the lower survival mode. Projecting our negative conditions onto others may seem to make things better, when the truth is that it is an unhealthy process for trying to make ourselves feel better. Negative projections often attach themselves to external movements and charge them with great power; something which has long been the bane of history.

We need to recognize that for far too long we have existed in what has been a pattern of human survival mode. And it goes something like this - we go to school, then we go to work, we may raise a family, go on vacation, enjoy ourselves and try to keep 'our heads above water' as they say. We do all these regular activities as an attempt to stay out of trouble, or out of crisis (generally!). We watch and listen to the news and shake our heads. We talk with our friends, our neighbors, and colleagues at work about the state of the world and again shake our heads. We go out for a drink, laugh at ourselves and the world. If we drink a little more than is good for us we may become nostalgic or even a little sad about 'what have I done?' and 'what am I really doing?' Then at the end of the day, or at the end of our lives, we shake our head again – 'what has it all been about?' We wonder and yet we never truly know. It has all been a great mystery, yet somewhere along the way we did enjoy ourselves – didn't we?

Even though so many of us now live in sophisticated 'civilized' societies, we still exhibit the same basic survival mode as did our ancestors for thousands of years. Our world around us has changed – yet *we* haven't changed sufficiently within it. We have not yet learnt to transcend the tiger. The tiger is us when we are in survival mode. It represents our base instincts and our fiendish and cunning ways of beating the law of the jungle. It is our fierce selves when we feel we must fight to remain alive – fight for our careers, our reputation, our status, our voice, etc. We are crying out in a tiger's roar to be heard, whilst the silence of the soul steps lightly and subtly deep within us.

With the increasing rise of technology we will not fade into obsolescence but rather will be pushed into exploring and updating our understanding of what it means to be human. As we activate our potentials within us we are likely to indirectly trigger others, perhaps unknown to us. We are not linear in this way but rather we are an integral organism. As the bardo years coalesce around us it is imperative we realize that our way ahead is to transcend our base instincts and to transform into soulful, compassionate, and loving human beings. In this there is true freedom.

about the author

Kingsley L. Dennis, PhD, is a full-time writer and researcher. He is the author of several critically acclaimed books including *The Sacred Revival, The Phoenix Generation, New Consciousness for a New World, Struggle for Your Mind, After the Car*, and the celebrated *Dawn of the Akashic Age* (with Ervin Laszlo). Kingsley is the author of numerous articles on social futures, new technologies, digital culture and new media, and conscious evolution.

Kingsley also runs a self-publishing imprint called Beautiful Traitor Books (www.beautifultraitorbooks.com). His most recent work of fiction is called *The Saffron Collectors.*

Kingsley is UK-born and currently lives in Andalusia, Spain. For more information, visit his website:

www.kingsleydennis.com

BOOKS DESERVING...

FOR INQUIRING MINDS...

about the publisher

Beautiful Traitor Books was founded in 2012 as an independent print-on-demand imprint to provide unusual and inspiring books for the discerning reader.

Our books are works that delve into various domains whether it is books for children, science fiction, social affairs, philosophy, theatre plays, or poetry. We have books translated into Spanish, French, Portuguese, Italian, and Hungarian.

All the books we publish seek to explore innovative and creative ideas. Many of them also tell a good story - stories that have different perspectives on life and on the human condition.

Beautiful Traitor Books is not only about offering the reader entertainment. We also seek to offer something that is like a nutrition; something of value that the reader can take away from the book. Good books function on more than one level. Put simply, we thrive on books that have the capacity to *shift* the reader.

Come and join the conversation – find out more at: www.beautifultraitorbooks.com

Made in the USA
San Bernardino, CA
27 January 2019